*An Introduction
to American
Literature*

Translated & Edited by

L. CLARK KEATING

& ROBERT O. EVANS

An Introduction to American Literature

Jorge Luis Borges

In collaboration with
Esther Zemborain de Torres

The University Press of Kentucky

Título del original en castellano:
Introduccion a la literatura norteamericana
Publicado en Buenos Aires, República Argentina,
por Editorial Columba
© by Columba S.A.C.E.I.I.F.A. 1967

ISBN: 0-8131-1247-8

Library of Congress Catalog Card Number: 73-147854

Editorial and Sales Offices: Lexington, Kentucky 40506

Contents

CONTENTS

Translator's & Editor's Preface

Jorge Luis Borges is an essayist, poet, critic, and writer of fiction with a wide and ever-increasing reputation. A visit to his personal library reveals a catholic taste in literatures of many lands, and a conversation with him is even more revealing. He seems to have read everything and to have forgotten nothing; he speaks several languages also. It is not to be wondered at, therefore, that he should have undertaken to write a history of American literature. He originally prepared his remarks for his own students, but it is plain that the book deserves a wider distribution. This English language edition was undertaken to make the work available to English-speaking students everywhere. Those who read it will discover that in this as in all the rest of his work Borges is a sound thinker as well as a witty and charming stylist.

Borges's *Introduction to American Literature* has many distinctions. First of all, it offers an outsider's view—that of a distinguished Argentine—of the literary achievement of the United States. We no longer live in an era when "American literature" must defend itself; nevertheless, it is pleasant to find the magnitude of the accomplishment so eloquently attested by a scholar from another culture. Borges shows the world how others see us. Where our ethnocentrism or parochialism may have distorted our perspective, he gently restores it. Where academic snobbery encourages us to concentrate on the literature of the intelligentsia, he reminds us of our vast popular literature and corrects our misconceptions concerning it.

It may be said that Borges's book is too terse. It is, as a matter of fact, the shortest history available to the student of American literature. It is not terse, however, in the sense of Emile Legouis's *A Short History of English Literature,* which is little more than a chronological compendium of authors, titles, and dates. Nor is it an outline for easy memorization by students preparing for their examinations. Every page contains a value judgment as well as important information.

Naturally there are omissions. Among the books discussed one may not always find his favorite work, although if the favorite is one of the best known it is likely to be there. Few authors important to the literary history of the United States are entirely neglected. The reader may note, however, the omission of Edward Taylor, the Puritan poet whose work has attracted renewed attention in our century, and George Santayana, the philosopher, whose novel *The Last Puritan,* exploring strains of Calvinism and hedonism in our culture and in himself, surely deserves a place in a more comprehensive survey. But on the whole Borges's omissions are not notable and may be explained in terms of the scope and size of the work.

The first half of the book is straightforward: that is, the authors are dealt with largely in chronological order, and what Borges has to say about Poe, Whitman, or Melville, for instance, will be quite familiar to the American student. But the second half of the book contains a number of surprises. Here Borges classifies writers in groups and abandons the survey method. The chapter headings give away the secret of his system, as they are no doubt intended to, but they do not reveal which writers are to be discussed. This system, similar to that of Legouis and Cazamian in their more comprehensive work, pulls together certain writers whom the reader may not hitherto have considered in relation to each other. For example, in the chapter on the expatriates we find Henry James, Gertrude Stein, F. Scott Fitzgerald, Ezra Pound, T. S. Eliot, E. E. Cummings, and Henry Miller, whereas Ernest Hemingway is considered in an earlier chapter on the narrators, the writers of prose fiction. Though Hemingway would normally be considered one of the expatriates, the principles of Borges's comparisons are seldom questionable because he brings to his task a sure esthetic sensibility.

Another, perhaps more striking, surprise in the second half of the book is the inclusion of esoteric categories and of many writers not ordinarily considered in literary histories. There is, for example, a section on the detective story, or *roman policier;* one on science fiction; and one on the Western, or cowboy story (what we sometimes call horse opera). In short, Borges accords to S. S. Van Dine, Erle Stanley Gardner, and the two writers known as Ellery Queen a place in our literary history. It is, of course, always debatable whether popular literature deserves critical recognition; but from the point of view of the outsider, the non-American, who reads American literature for enjoyment and for what it can tell him about the culture of the United States, the esoteric genres have a rightful place. Is it too much to suppose that they may some day come into their own, just as Wilkie Collins's *Moonstone* and Conan Doyle's Sherlock Holmes stories have assumed a place in English literature for as long, surely, as the language continues to be read?

Borges's guide to science fiction—a literature which, as he points out, is written for a very select audience—is as accurate and comprehensive as even an American reader new to the genre could wish. He ranges in a few short paragraphs from the magazines, for example, *Amazing Stories,* to Ray Bradbury, whose *Fahrenheit 451* has been a cinematic success.

The detective story is almost purely a product of the western democracies and is found largely in France, England, and the United States. Borges limits himself severely to the major American authors and does not draw comparisons. But when he comes to the Western he takes pains to point out essential differences between the cowboy story in the United States and its counterpart, the gaucho tale, in the Latin American countries.

At the end of his survey Borges gives us an all too brief sample of the oral poetry of the North American Indian, a subject entirely neglected in almost every other comparable study.

One finds here, then, a delightful guide to the literature of the United States which, despite its brevity, goes far beyond the scope of the ordinary textbook. Surely Borges himself would consider it a trifle, but if so it is an extremely useful and interesting trifle from the pen of one of the world's truly erudite men of letters.

Borges has a reputation for writing in a style that is as difficult as it is personal and charming. In this work, however, to the translator's surprise, his manner is simple and straightforward. It was a sheer delight to translate him.

Lexington, 1971

*An Introduction
to American
Literature*

Author's Preface

The limited space available in these outlines has obliged us to sum up nearly three centuries of literary activity in a single compact volume. There are in English many exhaustive histories of American literature, as seen from various points of view, not excluding the psychoanalytical. Plentiful also are those which try to make literature a branch of sociology. Such has not been our purpose; for us the essential ingredient is the esthetic one. In the United States, as in England, literary groups and coteries are less important than individuals; literary works come into being as the natural product of individual lives. We have preferred therefore to be guided by the appeal which the works have had for us. Furthermore, it goes without saying that the history of a literature cannot leave out of account the history of the country which produced it, and we have therefore included certain indispensable references.

It is perhaps not superfluous to mention that this compendium deals with topics which are not found in more comprehensive volumes, as for instance the detective story, science fiction, tales of the West, and the strange poetry of the American Indian.

Our fundamental purpose has been to encourage an acquaintance with the literary evolution of the nation which forged the first democratic constitution of modern times.

Buenos Aires, 1967

[1]

Origins

Valéry Larbaud, a French critic and a friend of Güiraldes,[1] remarked that beginning with Darío[2] and Lugones[3] Latin American literature has influenced that of Spain, while that of the United States has exerted and continues to exert an influence throughout the world, far beyond the vast domain of English.

Indeed, it is permissible to declare in Biblical fashion that Edgar Allan Poe begat Baudelaire, who begat the symbolists, who begat Valéry and that all the so-called civic poetry, or poetry of involvement, of our times is descended from Walt Whitman, whose influence is prolonged in Sandburg and Neruda.[4] To sketch, however lightly, the history of that literature is the purpose of these pages.

For a frontispiece we shall engrave, as a proper homage, the name of the famous Irish philosopher George Berkeley, the propounder of idealism. At the beginning of the eighteenth century Berkeley formulated in a poem a cyclical theory of history; he maintained that empires, like the sun, go from east to west ("Westward the course of empire takes its way") and that the last and greatest empire of history, conceived as a tragedy in five acts, would be that of America. He busied himself with a project for a seminary in the Bermudas which would prepare the rude English colonists and the Indians for that splendid and distant destiny. Later, when we come to speak of Jonathan Edwards, we shall return to Berkeley.

With pardonable exaggeration we shall say that the independence of America began on that morning in 1620 when the 102 Pilgrims of the *Mayflower* landed at a point on its eastern coast. They were, as is well known, nonconformists. Theologically they were Calvinists, adverse to the Anglican Church; politically they sided with Parliament and not with the king. Those who profess the doctrine of predestination are accustomed to believe, unless they are overcome by fear, that God has predestined them to glory rather than to hell; it was therefore inevitable that the colonists, avid readers of the Scriptures, should have identified themselves with the Israelites of the Exodus and should have seen themselves as a chosen people. They were guided by a messianic purpose which in Massachusetts finally led them to a theocracy.

An untamed continent surrounded them; they had to struggle against solitude, against the Indians and the forest, and finally against the armies of England and France. Like the first Christians they were hostile to the arts because they led men away from the fundamental business of salvation. In London in the middle of the seventeenth century the Puritans attacked theaters; hence the paradox in Shaw's title *Three Plays for Puritans*. Milton found it possible to upbraid Charles I for the strange sin of having devoted some of the days that preceded his execution to the profane reading of Shakespeare. In

Salem the Puritans accused many persons of witchcraft, for the Bible speaks of witches. It is curious to recall that it was enough to admit one's guilt in order to be declared innocent since the Devil would not allow those whom he possessed to confess their crime. The foolish who persisted in defending themselves were executed.

Now let us look at a few names.

The first historians of America were born in England: John Winthrop (1588–1649), who was governor of Massachusetts, drew up its constitution, which was a model for other colonies; William Bradford (1590–1657), who came on the *Mayflower,* was reelected governor for thirty years.

The son of Increase Mather, president of Harvard, Cotton Mather (1663–1728) was born in Boston. He provides us with the singular example of a tolerant Calvinist; he was sometimes inclined to deism. History links him with the witch trials of Salem, and he did not oppose the death sentences laid down by the courts, but he thought that the possessed could save themselves by prayer and fasting. His book *The Wonders of the Invisible World* relates and analyzes cases of diabolical possession. He was fluent in seven languages. An indefatigable reader and writer, he left to his children a library of some 2,000 volumes. He wrote more than 450 treatises, among them one in Spanish: *La fe del cristiano* (*The Faith of a Christian*). He wanted New England to be what Geneva and Edinburgh had failed to become—the leader of a world converted to Calvin's doctrines. He thought that the written word should always communicate something but that allusions and citations could increase its efficiency and embellish it "like the jewels that adorn the garments of a Russian ambassador."

A man of scientific curiosity, like [Jonathan] Edwards

who studied the habits of the spider, he was one of the first defenders of the use of vaccine.

Jonathan Edwards (1703–1758) was the most strenuous and complex of the Calvinistic theologians.[5] He was born in South Windsor, Connecticut. His vast work, explored today solely by historians, fills seventeen dense volumes in the London edition, and to these we must add those that contain his diary. He led and then disapproved of the religious movement known as the Great Awakening which, according to one of his biographers, began in ecstasy and mass conversions and degenerated, as occurs in so many similar cases, into unbridled license. William James cites him frequently in *The Varieties of Religious Experience*. Edwards was an energetic and effective preacher, not free from threatening postures. The title of the most famous of his sermons, "Sinners in the Hands of an Angry God," indicates his style. Let us quote from a typical paragraph: "The bow of God's wrath is bent, and the arrow made ready on the string, and justice bends the arrow at your heart . . . and nothing but the mere pleasure of God . . . keeps that arrow . . . from being made drunk with your blood." Metaphors of this sort have led to the supposition that Edwards was fundamentally a poet, frustrated by theology.

Endowed with a singular precocity, he entered Yale at the age of twelve and was ordained at fourteen. He carried on his ministry until 1750; at that date the scandals brought on by the Great Awakening obliged him to give up his pulpit. For a year, with the help of his wife and daughters, he was a missionary among the Indians. In 1757 he was named president of Princeton; he died a year later.

He preferred writing to reading; to writing, thinking and sometimes serene contemplation and fervent prayer. All he sought in books was a stimulus for his own activity. With the exception of Locke he seems to have read very few of his contemporaries. He knew the Platonic doctrine of eternal archetypes but nothing of Berkeley, although he agreed with him in the affirmation that the material universe is but an idea in the divine mind. Nor did he know Spinoza, who like himself identified God and nature as one and the same. In one of his last treatises Edwards says of God: "He is everything and he is alone."

The Calvinist doctrine that the Lord created the great majority of men for hell and but a few for glory seemed to him a terrible notion at first. However, during his youth he had a revelation, and he felt the doctrine to be "pleasing, clear and sweet"; surprisingly he found in it "an awful sweetness." In lightning and thunder, which had previously frightened him, he recognized, he tells us, the voice of God. Like Tertulian he thought that one of the joys of the fortunate would be the spectacle of the eternal torment of the damned. Rejecting free will, he extended to God the concept of necessity; he wrote that the acts of Jesus Christ were necessarily holy, although nonetheless to be extolled. Edwards belonged to the class who in Boston are called Brahmins, an allusion to the learned and priestly class of India.[6]

The first American poet of some renown, Philip Freneau (1752–1832), was of Huguenot descent.[7] His grandfather, a merchant, emigrated to New York in 1707, and Freneau was born there. His first writings were, like his last, of a satiric nature, but he also aspired to the epic. His complete works include a precocious epic on the prophet Jonah. He was a journalist, farmer, and sailor, "led on always by the witch of poverty." He sailed the tropic seas and knew the sea at first hand like Melville. During the Revolutionary War the ship that he commanded was captured by a British frigate, and the poet knew the prolonged hardships of a prison hulk in New York harbor.

An opponent of Washington, he was a partisan of Jefferson, but his complicated political activity does not concern us here.

More important are his lyrics. In the best known of his poems, "The Indian Burying Ground," he observes that we instinctively conceive of death as a sleep since we bury our dead in a reclining position, while the Indians think of it as a continuation of life since they bury theirs in a sitting position and provide them with bows and arrows for hunting in the other world. In this poem we find his most famous verse: "The deer and the hunter, a shade!" which recalls a hexameter in the eleventh book of the *Odyssey*.

Even more curious is the poem entitled "The Indian Student." Freneau tells the story of a young Indian who sells all his goods in order to acquire the mysterious learning of the white man. After painful wanderings he reaches the nearest university. He devotes himself first to the study of English and then to Latin; his professors foresee a brilliant future for him. Some maintain that he will be a theologian; others, a mathematician. Gradually the Indian, whose name is not revealed to us, begins to draw apart from his comrades and goes out walking in the woods. A squirrel, says the poet, distracts him from one of Horace's odes. Astronomy upsets him; the idea of the roundness of the earth and the infinity of space fills him with terror and uncertainty. One morning he goes away as silently as he came and returns to his tribe and his woods. The piece is at once a poem and a short story. Freneau tells it so well that no one can doubt that the facts were as described.

Freneau's occasionally allegorical style corresponds to the English poetry of the period, but its sensitivity is already romantic.

[2]

Franklin, Cooper, & the Historians

No history of American letters can omit Benjamin Franklin (1706–1790). His interests were many: typography, journalism, agriculture, hygiene, navigation, diplomacy, politics, pedagogy, ethics, music, and religion all attracted his energetic intelligence. He founded the first newspaper and the first periodical in America. Not one of the thousands of pages that he wrote was an end in itself but a means. The ten volumes of his work are circumstantial; he always wrote to accomplish an immediate end, far removed from pure literature. The practical nature of his work recalls Sarmiento,[8] who greatly admired him, but the lucid work of Franklin lacks the bright passion that illuminates *Facundo*.[9]

In his *Autobiography* are described the steps of his versatile and admirable career. He was born in Boston of humble parents and was self-taught. Thus in order to learn the art of prose he read, forgot, and reconstructed the essays of Addison. An official commission to purchase

materials for a printing press took him to London in
1724. At twenty-two he founded a religion, which did not
prosper, the essential precept of which was to do good. He
planned a city police force and a system of public light-
ing, and he drew up plans for paving the streets. He also
founded the first circulating library. He has been called,
not without a certain disdain, the apostle of common
sense. In the beginning he was opposed to a break between Great Britain and the colonies; later he became
a fervent partisan of American independence. In 1778
the Continental Congress named him minister pleni-
potentiary in Paris. The French saw in him a fine example
of the *homme de la nature:* Voltaire embraced him pub-
licly.

Like Poe, Franklin enjoyed mystifications. In 1773
the British government wished to oblige her colonies to
pay a tax; Franklin published in a London newspaper
an apocryphal decree by the King of Prussia that laid an
identical tax upon England since the island had been
colonized in the fifth century by tribes coming from
Germany.

One of his maxims was: "Never leave that till tomorrow which you can do today." Mark Twain was to
change this to: "Never put off till tomorrow what you can
do the day after tomorrow."

It is well known that Franklin invented the lightning
rod, an accomplishment which won him the famous trib-
ute from Turgot: "He snatched the lightning from the
sky, the scepter from the hand of the tyrant."[10]

Franklin was the first American writer to achieve
European fame—and even more renown as a philosopher,
in the sense that was given to this word in the eighteenth

century; the second was the novelist James Fenimore Cooper (1789–1851). Cooper's books, which today can count only on a decreasing juvenile audience, were translated into nearly all the languages of Europe and some of those of Asia. Balzac admired him, and Victor Hugo judged him superior to Scott; others were content to call him the Scott of America.

Cooper was born in Burlington, New Jersey. He spent his first years on a farm on the shores of Lake Otsego in close proximity to the woods and the Indians. He was educated in the local schools and then at Yale, from which he was expelled for a minor infraction. In 1805 he enlisted in the navy, where he served five years. In 1811 he gave that up to get married, and he settled down in Mamaroneck as a rural landowner. In 1819 chance or fate led to his reading a bad English novel with his wife. Cooper declared that he could write a better one. His wife challenged him to do so; the result was *The Precaution,* whose action is laid in England among society people. A year later he published *The Spy,* which takes place in America and foreshadows his later work. Cooper, like so many others, took some time to discover that what is interesting is not necessarily something far away but can be found in the here and now. The sea, the frontier, the sailor, the settler, and the Indian would be his themes. In five successive novels, of which the most widely circulated was *The Last of the Mohicans,* James Fenimore Cooper bequeathed to our imagination the stereotype of Leatherstocking, so called on account of his deerskin leggings. He is the backwoodsman incarnate; he is the white man who opens up the clearing in the forest and has identified himself with nature. He hates towns; he is brave, loyal, and skilful; his axe and rifle are infallible.

Beginning in 1826 Cooper lived for seven years in Europe. He was United States consul in Lyons; he had an opportunity to talk with his probable master, Sir Walter Scott, and with Lafayette. He wrote letters to the Frenchman which were gravely insulting to England and which, according to Andrew Lang, finally became equally irritating to the British lion and the American eagle. On his return home he resumed his work as a novelist[11] but was interrupted by litigation, the writing of satires, and by the compilation of his *History of the Navy* [*of the United States*]. His complete works fill thirty-three volumes.

Cooper's wordy prose, overstocked with words of Latin origin, has all the defects and none of the virtues of the style of the period. There is an irritating contrast between the violence of the deeds narrated and the slowness of his pen. [Robert Louis] Stevenson generously tells us that "Cooper is the wood and the wave."

A contemporary of Cooper was the historian and essayist Washington Irving (1783–1859). He was born in New York. Son of a wealthy merchant who had chosen the cause of independence, Irving was successively journalist, lawyer, and satiric author. In 1809 he concluded a burlesque history of New York, which he attributed to an imaginary pedantic Dutch historian, Diedrich Knickerbocker. In contrast to Cooper[12] he felt affection rather than hostility toward Europe. He traveled through England, France, Germany, and, after 1826, Spain. After eighteen years of absence he returned to his country and visited the frontiers of the West. In 1842 he was named United States minister to Spain. He lived for a long time in Granada, which he was to celebrate in *Tales of the Alhambra*. In his house, Sunnyside, he spent the last years of his life, devoting his time to the composition of historical works, the most ambitious of which is a monumental biography of Washington in five volumes.

He thought that his country lacked a romantic past and so he Americanized legends of other times and places. He retold, for instance, the story of the seven Christians pursued by an emperor, who lay down in a cavern with their dog and awakened, in the words of Gibbon, "after a momentary sleep of two centuries." They awakened in a Christian world; they were astonished to see the cross, which was previously a forbidden sign, on the gate of a city. Irving retained the dog but reduced the two hundred years to twenty and the seven sleepers to a farmer who goes out hunting and meets a stranger dressed in the ancient Dutch fashion. The latter takes him to a silent gathering where he is offered a drink with a strange taste. When he wakes up, the Revolutionary War has taken place. The name of Rip Van Winkle is well known in all countries where English is spoken.

Irving was not an investigator of the sources nor an original interpreter of the events to which he gave historical treatment. Thus his biography of Christopher Columbus is based on the work of Navarrete; his biography of Mahomet, on a similar book by the German Jewish orientalist Gustave Weil.

William Prescott (1796–1859) felt, like Irving, the peculiar enchantment of the hispanic world. He was born in Salem, Massachusetts. He belonged to that lettered class whom Boston calls the Brahmins, which has given us so many illustrious names. In 1843 he published his *History of the Conquest of Mexico,* a theme furnished him by Irving, and in 1847 his history *The Conquest of Peru.* He did not succeed in finishing the third volume of a history of Philip II.

Without slighting strict accuracy Prescott conceived of the writing of history as a work of art. He cared less about the sociological than about the dramatic. In the conquest of Peru by the Spaniards he saw the personal adventures of Pizarro, and in describing the explorer's death he reaches epic heights. His books, despite a certain romantic excess, read like good novels. Since his time certain details have been corrected, but no one can deny him the title of a great historian.

No less worthy of such a judgment is Francis Parkman (1823–1893), who was born in Boston. He was a man of precarious health, and like Prescott he had poor eyesight. He valiantly overcame these severe handicaps, dictating a good part of his work to others. His voluminous work is mainly of a historical nature. Two exceptions are the autobiographical novel *Vassall Morton* and *The Book of Roses,* which reflects his passion for flowers. He looked for his themes in America. He traveled through the various frontiers of the vast continent and got to know the life of the settlers and the Indians. The bloody rivalries between Great Britain, Spain, and France for dominion over the New World kept busy a pen that was as eloquent as it was severe. In this fashion he studied the wars in Canada, the missionary work of the Jesuits in the seventeenth century, and the victory of the pagan Iroquois over the converted tribes.

His best-known work relates the conspiracy of Pontiac, a famous chief of the Ottawas who, about the middle of the eighteenth century, sought an alliance with the French, used the arts of war and witchcraft against the British power, and was finally murdered.

Parkman died a year after Walt Whitman, but he is much closer in spirit to the Brahmins than to Whitman.

Let us read from one of his pages: "My political faith lies between two vicious extremes: democracy and absolute authority. I do not object to a good constitutional monarchy, but I prefer a conservative republic."

[3]

Hawthorne & Poe

The novelist and short-story writer Nathaniel Hawthorne (1804–1864) is more important than any of the writers studied thus far. He was born in the Puritan town of Salem, which would always attract him; his grandfather was one of the judges who occupied the bench at the witch trials; his father, a sea captain, died in the East Indies when Hawthorne was four years old. He graduated from college in Maine, where he struck up a friendship with [Franklin] Pierce and Longfellow. He later got a job in the customs service. After the death of his father the family led a strangely secluded life. Devoting themselves to the reading of the Scriptures and to prayer, they did not eat together and hardly ever spoke to each other. Their meals were left for them on a tray in the hall. Nathaniel spent his days writing fantastic tales; at nightfall he went out walking. This furtive existence lasted twelve years. In 1837 he wrote to Longfellow: "I have secluded myself from society and yet I never meant any such thing, nor dreamed what sort of life I was going to lead. I have made a captive of myself, and put me in a dungeon, and now I cannot find the key to let myself out —and if the door were open I should be almost afraid to come out." During this period Hawthorne wrote a story, "Wakefield," which in some ways reflects his own curious isolation. The hero, a worthy gentleman of London, abandons his wife one afternoon and takes up quarters around the corner from his own house, in hiding. After twenty years he returns without knowing why he had acted as he did. The story ends with these words: "Amid the seeming confusion of our mysterious world, individuals are so nicely adjusted to a system, and the systems to one another and to a whole, that by stepping aside for a moment, a man exposes himself to a fearful risk of losing his place forever. Like Wakefield, he may become, as it were, the Outcast of the Universe." The mysterious world of which Hawthorne speaks, ruled by inexplicable laws, is plainly Calvinistic predestination.

In 1841 Hawthorne took part for some months in the socialist colony of Brook Farm. In 1850 he published the most famous of his novels, *The Scarlet Letter;* the following year, *The House of the Seven Gables.* Franklin Pierce, on being elected president of the United States, named him consul in Liverpool. He afterward lived in Italy, where he wrote *The Marble Faun.* To the works already mentioned we must add various collections of short stories, of which the best known is perhaps *The Snow Image.*

By his feeling of guilt and his preoccupation with ethics Hawthorne is grounded in Puritanism; by his love of beauty and his fantastic invention he is related to another great writer, Edgar Allan Poe.

The son of poor actors, Edgar Allan Poe (1809–1849)

was born in Boston and was adopted by a merchant, John Allan, whose surname he took for his middle name. He was educated in Virginia and England; his English school was described by him in a fantastic tale, "William Wilson," whose hero dies on killing his double, or alter ego. Poe was expelled from the military academy at West Point. He made a precarious living by means of journalism; he incurred the enmity of his most illustrious contemporaries and accused Longfellow of plagiarism. From his youth onward alcohol and neuroses destroyed him. In 1836 he married his cousin Virginia Clemm, who was thirteen years of age; she died of tuberculosis in 1847. Poe died in a hospital in Baltimore; during the fever of his death agony he relived an atrocious episode from his book *The Narrative of Arthur Gordon Pym of Nantucket.* His life was short and unhappy, if unhappiness can be short.

Poe, a man of weak will and one torn by the most contradictory passions, professed a cult of reason and lucidity. Although he was fundamentally romantic, it nevertheless pleased him to deny the value of inspiration and declare that esthetic creativity stems from pure intelligence. In a work entitled "The Philosophy of Composition" he explains how he wrote his famous poem "The Raven" and analyzes, or pretends to analyze, the various steps in its composition. He began, he tells us, by imposing upon himself a limit of one hundred verses since a greater number would have destroyed the unified impression that he sought, while a smaller number would have been insufficient for its intensity. (As a matter of fact, "The Raven" contains 108 verses.) Then he thought that beauty is indispensable and that of all poetic moods the best is melancholy. The use of a refrain, because of its universality, seemed an efficient procedure. He thought that the sounds *o* and *r* are the most sonorous; the first word that occurred to him was *nevermore*. The immediate problem was to justify the monotonous repetition of that word by a rational being; an irrational one, but one capable of speech, could solve the problem. He thought of a parrot, but the raven impressed him by its greater dignity and melancholy. He then considered that there is nothing more melancholy than death and that the death of a beautiful woman is the poetic theme par excellence. Then the problem was to combine the two concepts—that of the lover, who weeps for the death of the loved one, and that of the raven, which at the end of each stanza repeats "Nevermore." This word, always the same, had to change meaning each time it was repeated. The only way was for the lover to ask questions which, trivial at the start, had to become extraordinary at the end. The lover, knowing in advance what the ominous responses would be, would torment himself by asking the questions. Finally he asks whether he will ever see his beloved again. The raven answers, "Nevermore." The stanza in which this occurs, one of the last in the poem, was the first one that the poet wrote. Insofar as versification is concerned, he looked above all else for originality. He combined verses of various meters and used both alliteration and rhyme.

How could he join together the lover and the raven? He thought of the fields or the woods, but an enclosed space seemed more suitable to concentrate the impression for which he was striving. He decided to situate the lover in a room filled with memories of the absent woman. How could the bird be made to enter? The idea of the window was inevitable. To justify the raven's seeking refuge a stormy night was appropriate; furthermore, the storm outside would contrast with the serenity of the room. The raven perches on the bust of Pallas Athena. Three reasons justify the bust: the contrast between the black plumage and the white marble; the appropriateness of such an image, which is the very symbol of learning, in a library; and the sonorousness of the name with its two open vowels. Half joking, the lover asks the raven what he is called on the plutonian shores of night. The raven replies, "Nevermore." The dialogue goes on, moving from the fantastic to the melancholic. The raven, sitting upon the marble bust, gradually makes an impression upon the lover and upon the reader also and prepares the denouement, which is not long in coming. The man understands that the bird can say only "Nevermore," but he deliberately tortures himself by asking questions that admit of this sad reply. Up to this point the composition is concrete, but the poet had decided that it should also express an allegory. The raven symbolizes the undying memory of interminable misfortune. Such is the analysis of the poem Poe offers us.

Poe's tales are divided into two categories which are sometimes intermingled: those of terror and those of intellect.[13] As for the first, someone accused Poe of imitating certain German romantics; he replied: "Terror is not of Germany, but of the soul." The second sort inaugurate a new genre, the detective story, which has conquered the entire world and among whose practitioners are Dickens, Stevenson, and Chesterton.

Edgar Allan Poe applied to his tales the same technique that he used in his verse; he believed that everything should be written with the last line in mind.

[4]

Transcendentalism

One of the most important intellectual events to occur in America was transcendentalism. It was not a sharply defined school but a movement; it included writers, farmers, artisans, businessmen, married women, and spinsters. Beginning in 1836, it flourished for a quarter of a century. Its center was the town of Concord in New England. It was a reaction against eighteenth-century rationalism, the psychology of Locke, and Unitarianism. This successor to orthodox Calvinism denied the Trinity, as its name implies, but affirmed the historical truth of the miracles performed by Jesus.

The roots of transcendentalism were multiple: Hindu pantheism, Neoplatonic speculations, the Persian mystics, the visionary theology of Swedenborg, German idealism, and the writings of Coleridge and Carlyle. It also inherited the ethical preoccupations of the Puritans. Edwards had taught that God can infuse the soul of the chosen with a supernatural light; Swedenborg and the cabalists, that the external world is a mirror of the spiritual. Such ideas influenced both the poets and the prose writers of Concord. The immanence of God in the universe was perhaps the central doctrine. Emerson reiterated that there is no being who is not a microcosm, a minuscule universe. The soul of the individual is identified with the soul of the world; physical laws are mingled with moral laws. If God is in every soul, all external authority disappears. All that each man needs is his own profound and secret divinity.

Emerson and Thoreau are now the most prominent names in the movement, which also influenced Longfellow, Melville, and Whitman.

The most illustrious individual example of the movement was [Ralph Waldo] Emerson (1803–1882). He was born in Boston, a son and grandson of Protestant ministers. He followed in the footsteps of his elders and after ordination accepted the pastorate of a Unitarian church in 1829. He was married the same year. In 1832, after a spiritual crisis which was doubtless influenced by the deaths of his wife and his brothers, he gave up the ministry. He thought that the day of formal religion had passed. Shortly afterward he took his first trip to England. He became acquainted with Wordsworth, Landor, Coleridge, and Carlyle, of whom he then thought himself a disciple. In reality they were essentially different.

Emerson always proclaimed himself an antislavery man; Carlyle was on the side of slavery. On his return to Boston he spent his time in travels and lectures, which acquainted him with the entire country. The lecture platform took the place of the pulpit. His fame spread not only in America but also in Europe. Nietzsche wrote that he felt himself so close to Emerson that he did not dare to praise him because it would have been like praising himself. Except for a few journeys Emerson always lived in Concord; in 1853 he married a second time. He died on April 27, 1882.

Emerson wrote that "arguments convince nobody" and that it is sufficient to state a truth for it to be accepted. This conviction gives his work a disconnected character. It abounds in memorable sayings, sometimes full of wisdom, which do not proceed from what has come before nor prepare for what is to come. His biographers say that before delivering a lecture or composing an essay he accumulated isolated sentences which he later strung together somewhat at random. Our exposition of transcendentalism sums up his doctrines. It is curious to observe that pantheism, which leads the Hindus to inaction, led Emerson to preach that there are no limits to what we can do since divinity is at the center of each of us. "You must know everything, dare everything." The breadth of his mind was astonishing. It is enough for us to recall the titles of the six lectures which he gave in 1845: "Plato, or the Philosopher"; "Swedenborg, or the Mystic"; "Shakespeare, or the Poet"; "Napoleon, or the Man of the World"; "Goethe, or the Writer"; "Montaigne, or the Skeptic." Of the twelve volumes of his work the most curious is perhaps the one which contains his poems. Emerson was a great intellectual poet. Poe, whom he called, not without disdain, the "jingle man," did not interest him. Here is the poem "Brahma":

> *If the red slayer thinks he slays,*
> *Or if the slain thinks he is slain,*
> *They know not well the subtle ways*
> *I keep, and pass, and turn again.*

> *Far or forgot to me is near;*
> *Shadow and sunlight are the same;*

The vanished gods to me appear;
And one to me are shame and fame.

They reckon ill who leave me out;
When me they fly, I am their wings;
I am the doubter and the doubt,
And I the hymn the Brahmin sings.

The strong gods pine for my abode,
And pine in vain the sacred Seven;
But thou, meek lover of the good!
Find me, and turn thy back on heaven.

The essayist, naturalist, and poet Henry David Thoreau (1817–1862) was born in Concord. At Harvard University he studied Greek and Latin; he was also interested
in the Orient, in history, and in the habits of the [Amer-
ican] Indians. He wanted to be self-sufficient, not making
promises to perform tasks to be completed at a later date;
he was a builder of boats and fences and an agricultural
surveyor. For two years he lived in the house of Emerson,
whom he resembled physically. In 1845 he retired to a
cabin on the shores of the solitary Walden Pond. His
days were spent in reading the classics, in literary composition, and in the precise observation of nature. He was
fond of solitude. On one of his pages we read: "I never
found the companion that was so companionable as solitude."

His most laconic biography was sketched by Emerson. "Few lives contain so many renunciations. He was
bred to no profession; he never married; he lived alone;
he never went to church; he never voted; he refused to
pay a tax to the state; he ate no flesh; he drank no wine;
he never knew the use of tobacco; and although a
naturalist he used neither trap nor gun. . . . He had no

temptations to fight against—no appetites, no passions, no taste for elegant trifles."

His work includes more than thirty volumes; the most famous is *Walden, or Life in the Woods,* published in 1854.

In 1849, a year before the appearance of Marx's *Communist Manifesto,* Thoreau had published the essay *Civil Disobedience,* which would influence the thought and destiny of Gandhi. The first lines affirm that the best government is that which governs least, and better still that which does not govern at all. And just as he rejected the idea of a standing army, he rejected the idea of a permanent government. He thought that government disturbed the natural development of the American people. The only obligation that he accepted was to do in each instance what seemed to him most just. He preferred to obey the right rather than the laws. He thought that reading newspapers was superfluous since to read the account of one fire or one crime is to know them all. He thought it useless to accumulate essentially identical cases.

He left this statement: "I long ago lost a hound, a bay horse and a turtle dove and I am still on their trail. Many travellers I have spoken to concerning them . . . I have met one or two who had heard the hound, and the tramp of the horse, and even seen the dove disappear behind a cloud, and they seemed as anxious to recover them as if they had lost them themselves." In these words, inspired perhaps by the recollection of some oriental fable, we feel Thoreau's melancholy more than in his verses. The historians of anarchism usually omit Thoreau's name, probably because his anarchism, like nearly all of his life, was of a negative and pacific sort.[14]

Although he is somewhat forgotten today, Henry Wadsworth Longfellow (1807–1882) was the most beloved poet of America during his lifetime. He was born in Portland, Maine. He held the chair of modern languages at Harvard University. His intellectual activity was untiring. He turned into English Jorge Manrique,[15] the Swedish poet Elias Tegner, the German and Provençal troubadours, and anonymous Anglo-Saxon poets. He versified passages from the *History of the Kings of Norway* by Snorri Sturluson. During the troubled days of the War of the Secession he consoled himself by making one of the best English translations of the *Divine Comedy,* enriched by curious notes. He wrote in hexameters the long poem *Evangeline* (1847), and in imitation of the meter of the Finnish epic *Kalevala* he wrote *Hiawatha* [1855], whose characters are Indians who foresee the coming of the white man. Many of the compositions of his book *Voices of the Night* [1839] won him the affection and admiration of his contemporaries, and they still endure in the anthologies. Reread now, they leave us the impression that all they lack is a final touch.

Far from transcendentalism, Henry Timrod (1828–1867) sang the hopes, the victories, the vicissitudes, and the final defeat of the South. He was born in Charleston, South Carolina, the son of a German bookbinder; he enlisted in the Confederate army, but tuberculosis deprived him of the military career that he so desired. In his verses there is fire and a classic sense of form. He died at the age of thirty-eight.

[5]

Whitman &
Herman Melville

Those who turn from the poetic work of [Walt] Whitman to his biography feel somewhat cheated. This is because the name Whitman really corresponds to two persons: the modest author of the work and its semidivine protagonist. To see the reason for this duality, let us begin by considering the first.

Walter Whitman (1819–1892), of English and Dutch descent, was born on Long Island. His father was a builder of frame houses, a trade which the son also followed. From childhood he was attracted by nature and books, and so he read the *Thousand and One Nights,* the works of Shakespeare, and, naturally, the Bible. In 1823 his family moved to Brooklyn. Whitman was a printer, a schoolteacher, a newspaperman, and, at twenty-one, the editor of the *Brooklyn Daily Eagle,* a job which he filled with a certain disenchantment. He lost the job in 1847. Until then his literary efforts had been insignificant; his biographers recall an antialcoholic novel and some mediocre verse. In 1848 he traveled with his brother to New

Orleans. There something happened. Some speak of an amorous adventure, others of a revelation which changed him profoundly. In 1855 he published the first edition of *Leaves of Grass,* which consisted of twelve poems and which earned him an enthusiastic and appropriate letter from Emerson. During the course of his life Whitman published twelve editions of *Leaves of Grass,* enriching it each time with new poems. After the third edition, which dates from 1860, the work contained compositions whose erotic frankness, perhaps never equaled, scandalized no few of his readers. During a long walk Emerson tried to dissuade him from this tendency; Whitman was to admit years later that his friend's reasons were irrefutable, but he would not let himself be convinced.

During the Civil War Whitman worked as a nurse in front-line hospitals and even on the field of battle. It is said that his very presence lessened the sufferings of the wounded. Early in 1873 an attack of paralysis prostrated him. By 1876 he was able to travel to Canada and the West, but in 1885 his health declined once more. Meanwhile his fame had spread throughout America and had reached Europe. He had many disciples who heeded his slightest word. He died in Camden [N.J.], poor but famous.

Whitman set himself the task of writing a messianic work, the epic of democracy in America. His favorite poet was Tennyson, but his own work required, so it seemed to him, a distinctive language: the oral English of the American streets and the frontier. He also inserted, usually in an incorrect manner, words from the Indian languages and from Spanish and French so that his epic might include all the regions of the continent. As for form, he rejected regular verse and rhyme and chose long, rhythmic stanzas, inspired by the psalms.

In previous epics a single hero was dominant: Achilles, Ulysses, Aeneas, Roland, or the Cid. Whitman, for his part, was determined that his hero should be all men. Of this he wrote:

*These are the thoughts of all men in all ages and lands—they
    are not original with me;
If they are not yours as much as mine, they are nothing, or
    next to nothing;
If they are not the riddle, and the untying of the riddle, they
    are nothing;
If they are not just as close as they are distant, they are nothing.*

*This is the grass that grows wherever the land is, and the
    water is;
This is the common air that bathes the globe.*

The Walt Whitman of the book is a plural personage; he is the author and he is at the same time each one of his readers, present and future. Thus certain apparent contradictions can be justified: in one passage Whitman is born on Long Island; in another, in the South. "Leaving Paumanok" begins with a fantastic biography: the poet tells of his experiences as a miner, a job that he never held, and describes the spectacle of herds of buffalo on the prairies, where he had never been.

"Salut au monde" compasses a total vision of the planet, with day and night occurring simultaneously. Among the many things that he sees are our pampas:

*I see the Wacho[16] crossing the plains, I see the incomparable
    rider of horses with his lasso on his arm;
I see over the pampas the pursuit of wild cattle.*

Whitman sang as if from a dawn; John Mason Brown has written that he and his followers represent the idea that America is a new event which poets should celebrate, while Edgar Allan Poe and his followers see it as a mere continuation of Europe. The history of American literature is to reflect the incessant conflict between these two conceptions.[17]

Like Mark Twain, Jack London, and so many other American writers, Herman Melville (1819-1891) led the kind of adventurous life of which the sedentary Whitman dreamed but which fate denied him. Melville was born in New York. The bankruptcy of his father, of old Scottish descent, left him in poverty at the age of fifteen. He was successively a bank clerk, a laborer, a schoolteacher, and, in 1839, a cabin boy. Thus began his long friendship with the sea. In 1841 he sailed on a whaler for the Pacific. He deserted in the Marquesas Islands, was captured by cannibals, and lived for some time with them. He married in 1847 and settled in New York. From there he went to a farm in Massachusetts, where he became the friend of Nathaniel Hawthorne, who influenced the writing of his major work, *Moby Dick*. During the last thirty-five years of his life he was employed in the customs service.

Melville's work consists of books about navigation and adventure, fantastic and satiric novels, poems, short stories, and the prodigious symbolic novel *Moby Dick*. Among his stories we shall recall *Billy Budd,* whose essential theme is the conflict between justice and the law; "Benito Cereno," which in some ways foreshadows *The Nigger of the Narcissus* of Conrad, and "Bartleby [the Scrivener]," the atmosphere of which is like that of the last books of Kafka. In the style of *Moby Dick* can be seen the influence of Carlyle and Shakespeare: there are

33

chapters conceived like the scenes of a drama. Unforgettable phrases abound: in one of the first chapters a preacher is spoken of who kneels in his pulpit and prays with such devotion that "he seemed kneeling and praying at the bottom of the sea." Moby Dick is the name of a white whale, the emblem of evil, and the mad search for the whale is the plot of the work. It is curious to note that the whale, as a symbol of the Demon,[18] figures in an Anglo-Saxon bestiary of the ninth century and that the notion that white is horrible constitutes one of the themes of Poe's *Arthur Gordon Pym*. Melville, in the very text of the work, denies that it is an allegory; the truth is that we may read it on two planes: as the story of imaginary doings and as a symbolic tale.

The importance and the profound novelty of *Moby Dick* were not immediately recognized. In 1912 the *Encyclopædia Britannica* saw in it nothing but a novel of adventure.

The five-year period from 1850 to 1855 is one of the most significant in American letters. In 1850 appeared Hawthorne's *The Scarlet Letter* and *Representative Men* by Emerson; in 1851, *Moby Dick;* in 1854, Thoreau's *Walden;* and in 1855, Walt Whitman's *Leaves of Grass.*

[6]

The West

As the United States grew westward and southward, as the war with Mexico and the conquest of the West expanded its already vast frontiers, a new generation of writers arose, quite alien to the Puritanism of New England and the transcendentalism of Concord. Longfellow and Timrod still belonged to the tradition of British letters; the new generation of writers, whose voices reach us from the Mississippi and the solitudes of California, did not even have to rebel against that tradition. The first was Samuel Langhorne Clemens (1835–1910), who gave world fame to the pseudonym Mark Twain.

Clemens was a typographer, a newspaperman, a river pilot, a second lieutenant in the armed forces of the South, a prospector, a writer of humorous pieces, a lecturer, the editor of a newspaper, a novelist, editor, businessman, doctor *honoris causa* of American and English universities, and, during the last years of his life, a celebrity. He was born in Florida, a small town in Missouri. Its population was one hundred souls; Mark Twain boasted of having increased it by 1 percent, "a thing that many distinguished persons could not have done for their country."

Shortly thereafter his family moved to Hannibal [Missouri] on the banks of the Mississippi. Throughout his life he was haunted by the image and nostalgia of the river, which inspired his best books, *Tom Sawyer* and *Huckleberry Finn*. At twenty he conceived of a plan for exploring the sources of the Amazon, but on reaching New Orleans he decided to become a river pilot on the Mississippi. This period revealed to him the most diverse of human types; years later he would write: "Each time in fiction or in history I meet a well-defined personality I am personally interested in him, for we know each other already, because we met on the river." In 1861 the War of the Secession closed the river to navigation; Mark Twain, after some two weeks of military activity, accompanied his brother to the West. They made the long journey in a stagecoach. In San Francisco, California, Bret Harte and the humorist Artemus Ward initiated him into literature; from then on he used the pseudonym Mark Twain, which in the language of river pilots means "two fathoms." In 1865 a short yarn, "The Celebrated Jumping Frog of Calaveras County," gave him continental fame. Later would come the lecture tours; the trips to Europe, the Holy Land, and the Pacific; the books which would be translated into all languages; his marriage, prosperity, and economic reverses; the death of his wife and children; renown, secret solitude, and pessimism.

For his contemporaries Mark Twain was a humorist, a man whose slightest deeds were made known by telegraph from one end of the planet to the other. These jokes, reaching us now, seem a little tired. There remains and will remain, however, *Huckleberry Finn,* the starting point, according to Hemingway, of the entire American novel. Its style is oral; the leading characters, a mischievous boy and a runaway Negro, sail a raft at night on the broad waters of the Mississippi and thus depict to us life in the South before the Civil War. Moved by a generous sentiment which he does not quite understand, the boy helps the slave, but he is troubled by remorse for becoming an accomplice in the flight of a man who is the property of a woman in the town. From this great book, which abounds in admirable evocations of mornings and evenings and of the dismal banks of the river, there have arisen in time two others whose outline is the same, *Kim* (1901) by Kipling and *Don Segundo Sombra* (1926) by Ricardo Güiraldes. *Huckleberry Finn* was published in 1884; for the first time an American writer used the language of America without affectation. John Mason Brown has written: "*Huckleberry Finn* taught the whole American novel to talk."

Halley's comet was shining in the sky when Mark Twain was born; he predicted that his days would not end until the comet returned. And so it happened: in 1910 the comet returned and the man died.

The novelist Howells wrote: "Emerson, Longfellow and Holmes—I knew them all. . . . They were like one another . . . but Clemens was sole, incomparable, the Lincoln of our literature."

The vastness of the desert regions won for the United States in the West obliged the settlers to engage in the most varied of activities. Thus Bret Harte (1836–1902), born in Albany [N.Y.], the friend and protector of Mark Twain, was successively schoolmaster, drug clerk, miner, messenger, typographer, reporter, author of short stories, regular contributor to the *Golden Era*, and, after 1868, the editor of the important magazine *The Overland Monthly*. In its pages appeared those short, pathetic masterpieces "The Luck of Roaring Camp," "The Outcasts of Poker Flat," and "Tennessee's Partner," which the author was to collect under the title *The California Sketches* and which were perhaps the first revelation of the West. A humorous poem, "The Heathen Chinee," made him famous from the Pacific to the Atlantic. In 1878, at his request, he was appointed consul in the city of Crefeld, in Prussia, and later in Glasgow. He spent his last years in London.

Bret Harte and Mark Twain, typical writers of the West, came from other regions; but John Griffith London (1876–1916), who took the name Jack London, was born in San Francisco, California. His destiny was no less irregular than that of the other two: he knew poverty; he was a farmhand, a ranch hand, a newspaper vendor, a vagabond, a leader of a gang, and a sailor. Street begging and prison were not outside his experience. He decided to educate himself; in three months he completed a two-year course of study and entered the University of California. In 1897 gold was discovered in Alaska. London took off and in the dead of winter crossed the Chilkoot Pass. He did not find the treasure he was looking for, and with two companions he tried to cross the Bering Strait in an open boat. In 1903 he published his novel *The Call of the Wild,* of which one and a half million copies were sold. It is the story of a dog that had been a wolf and that finally becomes one again. A previous book, *The God of His Fathers,* had not achieved an equal success. During the Russo-Japanese war in 1904 London was sent out as a correspondent. He died at forty, leaving behind some fifty volumes. Of these we shall mention *The People of the Abyss,* for which he personally explored the low quarters of London; *The Sea Wolf,* whose leading character is a sea captain who preaches and practices violence; and *Before Adam,* a novel on a prehistoric theme, whose narrator recovers in fragmentary dreams the troubled days through which he had lived during a previous incarnation. Jack London also wrote admirable adventure stories and some fantastic tales, among which is "The Shadow and the Flash," which tells of the rivalry and the final duel of two invisible men. His style is realistic, but he re-creates and exalts a reality of his own. The vitality which permeated his life also permeates his work, which will continue to attract young readers.

Frank Norris (1870–1902) was born in Chicago, but his work belongs to the West. He was educated in San Francisco, studied medieval art in Paris, and was successively a war correspondent in South Africa and in Cuba. His first works were romantic, but toward the end of the nineteenth century he was converted to Zola's naturalism and published the novel *McTeague* (1899), the scene of which is laid in the low quarters of San Francisco. He left an unfinished trilogy whose protagonist is wheat, from its production to the speculation on the commodity exchange and its exportation to Europe. In contrast to his master, who documented his work in libraries,[19] Frank Norris, before he undertook the composition of his trilogy, worked as a laborer on a California farm. He believed that certain impersonal forces—wheat, railroads, the law of supply and demand—are more important than the individual and end by dominating him, but he also believed in immortality. He is considered a precursor of Theodore Dreiser, whose first novel, *Sister Carrie,* he helped to publish.

[7]

Three Poets of the Nineteenth Century

The biography of Sidney Lanier (1842–1881) is less memorable than his poetic theory and his application of that theory. Of Scottish and Huguenot ancestry, he was born in the town of Macon, Georgia. Music was his first love; during the last years of his life he distinguished himself as a flutist. In the Civil War he fought for four years in the Confederate army and was taken prisoner by northern troops. He was already tubercular; the privations of captivity, in which his only solace was the flute, aggravated his disease. In one of his letters we read: "Pretty much the whole of life has been merely not dying." A judgeship, law, music, the compilation of romantic books, and the study of Anglo-Saxon poetry kept his days occupied. In 1879 he held the professorship of English poetry at Johns Hopkins University.

Verlaine has written: *de la musique avant toute chose* ("music before all else"), but Lanier went even further; he held that instrumental music and verse are fundamentally identical, and he applied to the second the methods and rules of the first.[20] He declared that in prosody the important thing is time, not stress. To his musical preoccupation he added a metaphysical one, which relates him to certain English poets of the seventeenth century. Lanier accused Whitman of confusing quantity with quality and wrote: "Whitman's argument seems to be that because a prairie is wide debauchery is admirable, and because the Mississippi is long every American is God." He did not succeed in being a great poet, perhaps because his wish to write in order to illustrate a predetermined theory dulled his inspiration. He has left beautiful stanzas, however. To his treatises on prosody we should add his autobiographical novel, *Tiger Lilies* (1867), and a study of Shakespeare and his precursors.

In his time John Greenleaf Whittier (1807–1892) enjoyed in the North a popularity almost equal to that of the versatile and erudite Longfellow. He was born in Haverhill, Massachusetts. Like his forebears he belonged to the Society of Friends, commonly called Quakers, who since the seventeenth century have eschewed violence and have participated in wars only as nurses, although sometimes on the field of battle. He was what we would call today a dedicated poet; in sonorous verse he advocated the abolition of slavery. As happens in such cases, the triumph of the cause in question has diminished our interest in his work. In anthologies his long poem *Snowbound* survives; it describes vividly a blizzard in New England. Whittier was so American that he needed to use no Americanisms to prove it.

It is customary to say of Emily Dickinson (1830–1886) that she was the last of the transcendentalists. She was born in the town of Amherst, Massachusetts, where she spent nearly all her days. Her father was a Puritan of the old school; Emily wrote that his heart was "pure and terrible" and that she loved him with a reverence that excluded all intimacy. Edward Dickinson was a lawyer; he gave his daughter books as presents, with the curious recommendation not to read them lest they upset her. The Puritan theocracy no longer existed, but it had bequeathed a style of life to its descendants and a habit of rigor and solitude. At age twenty-three, during a brief visit to Washington, Emily met a young preacher and they fell in love immediately, but on learning that he was married, she refused to see him again and returned home. She was pretty and did not stop smiling; she sought refuge in epistolary friendships, in dialogue with members of her family, in the faithful reading of a few books —Keats, Shakespeare, the Scriptures—in long walks in the country accompanied by her dog, Carlo, and in the composition of brief poems, of which she was to leave about a thousand, the publication of which did not interest her. Sometimes for years at a time she never crossed the threshold of her house. In a letter she writes: "You ask of my companions. Hills, sir, and the sundown, and a dog large as myself, which my father bought me. They are better than beings because they know, but do not tell; and the noise in the pool at noon excels my piano." In another: "I had no portrait, now, but am small like a wren, and my hair is bold like the chestnut burr; and my eyes, sherry in the glass which the guest leaves."

Despite obvious differences the poetic work of Emerson and that of Emily Dickinson have an affinity for each other. We should not attribute that affinity to the direct influence of the first but to the fact that they shared a Puritan environment. Both were intellectual poets; both disdained or were indifferent to the sweetness of verse. Emerson's intelligence was more lucid; Emily Dickinson's sensitivity perhaps more refined. Both abound in abstract words. A life's work which consists of a thousand fragments and which was not written to be printed suffers fatally from unevenness, but in its best pages mystic passion and inventive faculty come together, as in those English poets of the seventeenth century whom Johnson dubbed metaphysical and who correspond in some ways to the conceptists of Spain. Emily can take a commonplace—for instance, the idea that man is dust—and transmute it into delicate poetry. Thus she writes: "This quiet dust was gentlemen and ladies." In another poem she declares that only someone who has been defeated knows victory. In another place: "The only news I have are bulletins which reach me all day from Immortality. The only spectacles that I see are tomorrow and today, perhaps Eternity. I meet no one but God, my only street is existence; when I have explored it if there is any other news or any admirable spectacle I shall then tell you about it." In addition to the amorous episode already mentioned, there must have been another, for she wrote:

My life closed twice before its close:
It yet remains to see
If immortality unveil
A third event to me

So huge, so hopeless to conceive
As these that twice befell:
Parting is all we know of heaven,
And all we need of hell.[21]

[8]

The Narrators

William Sidney Porter (1862–1910), whose name for fame is O. Henry, was born in Greensboro, North Carolina. He was a drug clerk and then a journalist; like Juan Manuel de Rosas[22] he read the dictionary from the first page to the last, thinking thus to acquire the sum of human knowledge. About 1895, while a cashier in the Bank of Texas in Austin, he was accused of embezzlement and fled to Honduras, from where he returned when he heard that his wife was dying. He witnessed her death agony and endured three years of imprisonment. Edgar Allan Poe had maintained that every short story should be written with a view to its final outcome; O. Henry exaggerated this doctrine and thus arrived at the trick story, the tale whose final line springs a surprise. Such a procedure in the long run has something mechanical about it; nevertheless O. Henry has left us more than one brief, pathetic masterpiece, such as "The Gift of the Magi" included in the collection called *The Four Million* (1906). His work, which includes several novels and a hundred-odd stories, mirrors a New York lost in nostalgia and a West of old adventurers.

The novels, short stories, and dramatic pieces of Edna Ferber, who was born in Kalamazoo, Michigan, in 1887, are intentionally constituted as a broad epic of the United States and cover successive generations and various regions. The characters of *Show Boat* (1926) are itinerant gamblers and actors on the Mississippi; *Cimarron* (1929) describes in a romantic manner the winning of the West; *American Beauty* (1931), the trials and tribulations of a group of immigrant Poles; *Come and Get It* [1935], the lumbering industry of Wisconsin; *Saratoga Trunk* (1941), the tangled intrigues of a crowd of adventurers at the spa of Saratoga; *Giant* (1950), the growth of Texas. A number of her works have been made into movies.

The young writer Stephen Crane (1872–1900) was born in Newark, New Jersey. A contemporary and friend of H. G. Wells, who recalls him with admiration in his autobiography, Crane left at least two short masterpieces: the story "The Open Boat" and the novel *The Red Badge of Courage*. The theme of the latter is the War of the Secession as lived by a recruit who cannot tell whether he is a coward or a man of courage until action has put him to the test. The lonesomeness of each soldier during battle, his total ignorance of the overall strategy, his alternation between courage and despair, his surprise on finding out how short was the infantry charge that seemed to him interminable and how little ground was gained, "the valiant dream of tired men"—these are some of the many subjects contained in this vivid book. Its only defect is a certain excess of metaphors.

Crane was a journalist in Mexico and a war correspondent in Greece and Cuba. He died of tuberculosis in Germany. The twelve volumes of his work include two books of poetry: *Black Riders* and *War Is Kind*.

45

Crane's influence has been felt in certain esthetic habits of Theodore Dreiser (1871–1945), but this influence is accidental.[23] Crane is vivid and brief and tends toward the epigrammatic; Dreiser gets his effects, which are undeniably considerable, by insistence, accumulation, and volume. The former imagined reality; the latter impresses us as having studied it. The son of austerely religious German immigrants, Dreiser was born in Terre Haute, Indiana. The poverty of his first years led him to long for wealth and the power that it gives, a longing which defines the heroes of the novels *The Financier, The Titan,* and *The Stoic.* He practiced journalism in various parts of the country. The reading of Balzac, Spencer, and Huxley led him to conceive of existence as a dramatic but senseless conflict between vast forces. In 1900 he published the novel *Sister Carrie,* which was taken out of circulation. This unpleasant episode and the hostility and lack of understanding of the critics embittered him. His later works—*Jennie Gerhard, The Genius, The Bulwark,* and *An American Tragedy*—accentuate the realism of his first ones and display an increasing contempt for beauty and even for correctness of style. He thought that in view of the chaotic nature of the universe no moral satisfaction `s possible and that it is our duty to be rich or try to be. His work reflects this idea with a desperate and powerful sincerity. About 1927 he was converted to communism and visited Russia. Despite the harshness and violence of his doctrines he was a romantic at heart.[24]

The industrialist Sherwood Anderson (1876–1941) discovered his literary vocation late in life, when he was nearly forty. He was born in Camden, Ohio, a town which was to inspire his most lasting work. He was a soldier in the war in Cuba. About 1915 he settled in Chicago, which was just beginning to be a literary center. Under the influence of the poet Carl Sandburg he wrote his first novel, *Windy McPherson's Son,* whose theme is the unsatisfied man who escapes from his surroundings in search of truth. This was the theme of all his later work, and it reflects his own experience. An English critic has observed that Sherwood Anderson thinks in terms of episodes, real or imagined; this would explain why his short stories are generally superior to his novels. The collection of stories entitled *Winesburg, Ohio* (1919), is still regarded as his major work despite the uneven quality of certain pages.

He was married four times; for many years he was at one and the same time editor of a Republican and a Democratic newspaper in Marion, Virginia.

About 1930, the year in which he won the Nobel Prize, Sinclair Lewis (1885–1951) was his country's most famous novelist. He was born in Sauk Center, Minnesota. His extensive work abounds in satire; there were some who thought that the prize of the Swedish Academy was awarded less in Mr. Lewis's favor than in opposition to the society he castigated. In 1926 Lewis had turned down the Pulitzer Prize. Without failing to be quite human and full of plausible contradictions, the heroes of his books are also types. Babbitt is the businessman living among more or less conventional friendships and affections, yet consumed by loneliness; Elmer Gantry is the charlatan clergyman, unscrupulous and greedy, who wavers between cynicism and hypocrisy; Arrowsmith is the physician devoted to his profession; Dodsworth, the wealthy and weary man who would like to revitalize himself in

Europe. *Main Street* (1920) describes the tedium of existence in a town forgotten on the vast agricultural plain of the [Middle] West.

Lewis was a socialist; about 1906 he participated in the Utopian colony of Helicon Home, founded by Upton Sinclair. Before attempting the realistic novel, he tried the theater, newspaper work, and romantic fiction. An individualist in the beginning, then a socialist, he was essentially and irreparably a nihilist.

John Dos Passos, whom Jean Paul Sartre has called the major writer of his time, was born in Chicago in 1896 of Portuguese and American origin.[25] He went to Harvard and was a soldier in the First World War and then a war correspondent in Spain. He traveled through France, Mexico, and the Near East. His work is varied, dazzling, and in a certain sense anonymous. His characters count for less than the crowds of people about them; the author's intimate feelings are relegated to sections which he calls the camera eye and are crushed by outward circumstances. According to the unanimous opinion of the critics his major work is the trilogy *U.S.A.*, which leaves a final impression of sadness and futility since it suffers from a lack of passion and faith. Dos Passos has brought to the novel the typographical methods of the newspaper as well as its miscellaneous and superficial character. Less important than his prose are his dramatic essays and his poetry. We do not know whether his work will last, but his technical importance is undeniable.

In this chapter we have spoken of writers of unquestionable talent; now we reach a man of genius, although a wilfully and perversely chaotic one: William Faulkner (1897–1964). He was born in Oxford, Mississippi; in his vast work the provincial and dusty town, surrounded by the shanties of poor whites and Negroes, is the center of a county to which he has given the name Yoknapatawpha,[26] an appellation of presumably Indian origin. During the First World War Faulkner enlisted in the Royal Canadian Air Force; then he was a poet, a journalist connected with New Orleans publications, and the author of famous novels and movie scenarios. In 1950 he was awarded the Nobel Prize. Like the now forgotten Henry Timrod, Faulkner represents in American letters that feudal and agrarian South which after so many sacrifices and so much courage was defeated in the Civil War, the most ferocious and bloody conflict of the nineteenth century, not excepting the Napoleonic campaigns and the Franco-Prussian War. To Timrod were given the initial hopes and victories; Faulkner describes in an epic manner the disintegration of the South through many generations. Faulkner's hallucinatory tendencies are not unworthy of Shakespeare, but one fundamental reproach must be made of him. It may be said that Faulkner believes his labyrinthine world requires a no less labyrinthine technique. Except in *Sanctuary* (1931) his story, always a frightful one, is never told to us directly; we must decipher it and deduce it through tortuous, inward monologues, just as we do in the difficult final chapter of Joyce's *Ulysses*. Thus in *The Sound and the Fury* (1929) the degeneration and tragedy of the Compson family is provided by the slow and provocative description of four distinct hours, reflecting what is felt, seen, and remembered by three characters, one of them an idiot. Other major novels by Faulkner are *As I Lay Dying* (1930), *Light in August* (1932), *Absalom! Absalom!* (1936), and *Intruder in the Dust* (1948).

The son of a rural Illinois doctor, Ernest Hemingway (1898–1961) was born in Oak Park, Illinois. In his childhood he was influenced by long vacations on the shores of Lake Michigan and in the nearby woods. He shared with his father the pleasures of hunting and fishing. He refused to study medicine and became a journalist before enlisting as a soldier in the Italian army in the First World War.[27]

He was seriously wounded and received a decoration. Around 1921 he settled in Paris, where he became the friend of Gertrude Stein, Ezra Pound, Ford Maddox Ford, and Sherwood Anderson. He parodied the last named in the novel *Torrents of Spring* (1926). That same year *The Sun Also Rises* revealed him as one of the outstanding writers of his generation. In 1929 he published *A Farewell to Arms*. He was a war correspondent in the Near East and in Spain and a lion hunter in Africa. These varied experiences are reflected in his work. He did not seek out such experiences for literary purposes; they interested him deeply. In 1954 the Swedish Academy awarded him the Nobel Prize in Literature for his exaltation of man's most heroic virtues.[28] Overcome by his inability to go on writing, and suffering from insanity, he killed himself in 1961. It grieved him to have devoted his life to physical adventures rather than the pure and simple exercise of the intelligence.

Three Stories and Ten Poems (1923) and *In Our Time* (1925) correspond to memories of his childhood in the Michigan woods; *The Sun Also Rises,* to his bohemian years in Paris; the fourteen stories of *Men without Women* (1927), to the courage of bullfighters, boxers, and gangsters; the novel *A Farewell to Arms,* to his military experiences in Italy and to postwar disillusionment; *Death in the Afternoon* (1932), to bullfighting and the concept of death; the fourteen stories of *Winner Take Nothing* (1933), to his nihilism. In *The Green Hills of Africa* (1935) analysis of the art of writing alternates with observations which were later to inspire the stories "The Snows of Kilimanjaro" and "The Short Happy Life of Francis Macomber." After 1937 he was in search of moral affirmations, and in 1940 he published *For Whom the Bell Tolls,* a novel of the Spanish Civil War, whose title comes from one of the sermons of John Donne. *Across the River and into the Trees* (1950) tells of the love of two persons of unequal ages; *The Old Man and the Sea,* of the courageous and solitary struggles of an old man with a fish.

Hemingway, like Kipling, saw himself as a craftsman, a scrupulous artisan. For him the fundamental thing was to justify himself before death by a task well done.

[9]

The Expatriates

The first and most illustrious of the expatriates was Henry
James (1843–1916), the younger brother of the philosopher and psychologist William James (1842–1910), who
founded the school of pragmatism. Their father wanted
his sons to be citizens of the world in the manner of the
Stoics, avoiding the acquisition of premature habits of
conduct or thought. He did not believe in schools or universities; and for this reason William and Henry were
educated in Italy, Germany, Switzerland, England, and
France by private tutors, taking whatever courses interested them. About 1875, after brief law studies at Harvard, Henry left New England for good and settled in
Europe. By 1871 he had published his first novel, *Watch
and Ward;* in 1877 appeared *The American,* whose hero,
a man deeply wronged, gives up an easy vengeance in the
last chapter. James rewrote this book; in one version the
outcome is due to the nobility of the hero's character; in
the other, to a feeling that vengeance would link him yet
more closely to his enemies, whom he wants to forget.

Henry James was the personal friend of Flaubert,

Daudet, Maupassant, Turgenev, Wells, and Kipling. At the beginning of our century his situation was curious; everyone praised him, everyone called him a master, yet nobody read him. Tired of fame, he wanted popularity and sought it by writing plays, but with little success. In 1915 he became a British citizen to show his solidarity with the cause of the Allies since the United States had not yet entered the war. He was born in New York; his ashes rest in a cemetery in Massachusetts.

In contrast to Emerson and Whitman, James maintained, under the influence of Flaubert, that an old and complex civilization is indispensable for the cultivation of art. He regarded the American as morally superior to the European but intellectually simpler. The theme of his first works (to one of which we have referred) is the contrast between these two human types. Lambert Strether, the Puritan hero of the novel *The Ambassadors* (1903), takes a trip to Paris to save young Chad from debauchery. He does so at the request of the boy's widowed mother, Mrs. Newsome, whom he is secretly courting. He ends by giving in to the enchantment of the city and realizing that his life so far has been a failure. He returns to America, still incapable of living fully and of forgetting the past. Altogether different is the novel *What Maisie Knew,* of 1897, which lets us glimpse a series of awful deeds through the mind of a child, who tells them without suspecting their true nature.

James's stories are no less compact than his novels and far more interesting reading. The most famous, *The Turn of the Screw,* is purposely ambiguous and full of subtle horror; it has lent itself to three interpretations, all of them justified by the text. "The Jolly Corner" is the story of an American who returns after years of absence to his home in New York. He walks through it and pursues through the shadows a human form which runs away. This sorrowing and mutilated figure, which resembles him, is the man he would have been if he had stayed in America. "The Figure in the Carpet" relates the case of a novelist in whose vast work there is a central purpose, invisible at first like the design in an intricate Persian rug; the writer dies and a group of critics spend their lives trying to find the secret pattern, which they will never succeed in doing. In "The Lesson of the Master" a great novelist also appears; he dissuades his secretary from marrying a young Australian heiress lest the marriage take him away from the work that he ought to do. The secretary allows himself to be persuaded; the master marries the Australian, and it is not certain whether his advice had been sincere or not. "The Tree of Knowledge" is the story of a man trying to prevent the son of a sculptor friend from discovering the extraordinary mediocrity of his dead father; in the last paragraph we learn that the son had always despised his father's work. It is symptomatic of James that in "The Great Good Place" he should show us paradise in the form of an expensive sanatorium; evidently he could not conceive of any other sort of happiness. "The Private Life" has two heroes: one is a character who, when he is not presiding over a congress or receiving delegations or delivering an eloquent speech, disappears completely because he is nobody; the other is a poet who leads an active social life and yet produces a considerable work. The narrator shows that the poet, like Pythagoras, has mastered the art of being in two places at the same time. He is at a party and he is at the same time in his room writing. From the perplexities of the American in Europe James went on to the theme of the perplexity of man in the universe. He had no faith in an ethical, philosophical, or religious solution to essential problems; his world is already the inexplicable world of Kafka. Despite the scruples and delicate complexities of James his work suffers from a major defect: the absence of life.

Gertrude Stein (1874–1946) is perhaps less important for her work, unreadable at times and intentionally obscure, than for her personal influence and her curious literary theories. She was born in Allegheny, Pennsylvania, was a student of the psychologist William James, and studied medicine and biology. In 1902 she settled in Paris. She accompanied her brother Leo, who was knowledgeable about painting, and this linked her with Picasso, Braque, and Matisse, who in time became famous. Their pictures suggested to her that colors and forms can impress us in a fashion altogether distinct from the themes they represent. Gertrude Stein resolved to apply this principle to words, which were never mere ideological symbols for her. The lectures that she gave in the United States after being away for thirty years explain her philosophy of composition and are based on the esthetic theories of William James and on the Bergsonian concept of time. She maintained that the purpose of literature is to express the present moment, and she compared her own technique with that of the cinema: no two scenes on the screen are exactly alike; but sequentially presented, they provide the eye with a fleeting continuity. She was prodigal with verbs and avoided the use of nouns, which might interrupt that continuity. She influenced three generations of artists, among whom we can name Sherwood Anderson, Hemingway, Ezra Pound, Eliot, and Scott Fitzgerald. Her work consists mainly of *Three Lives* (1909), a book of verse (*Tender Buttons*, 1914), *How to Write* (1931), and *The Autobiography of Alice B. Toklas* (1933).

Francis Scott Key Fitzgerald (1896–1940) was born in Saint Paul, Minnesota, of an Irish Catholic background. He was educated at Princeton, which he left in 1917 to enlist in the American army. One of his first ambitions was to be brave, but the war ended before he could see action. His whole life was a search for perfection: he sought it in the concepts of youth, beauty, aristocracy, and a wealth which would permit men a greater generosity, a greater degree of disinterestedness, and a more spontaneous courtesy. His characters correspond to his personal experiences, his first illusions, and his final disenchantment. In his many-faceted work two books stand out. *The Great Gatsby* (1925) is the story of a man trying in vain to recover a youthful love which has been transmuted into a longing for the old American dream of a new world. Daisy and Buchanan, her husband, the very rich, the invulnerable, remain united; Gatsby is destroyed. Technically superior, *Tender Is the Night* (1934) analyzes the life of an expatriate who returns to America to hide his inward failure. More than any other writer of his generation, Scott Fitzgerald represents the years which followed the First World War.

A distant relative of Longfellow, Ezra Loomis Pound (b. 1885) has aroused the most contradictory of opinions. For Eliot, who has called him the best craftsman—*il miglior fabbro*—he is a master; for Robert Graves, a pretender. He was born in Hailey, Idaho, and did graduate work at the University of Pennsylvania, where he taught. In 1908 he published his first book, *A Lume Spento,* in Venice. From 1908 to 1920 he lived in London. It was his custom to appear in literary circles dressed like a cowboy in order to call attention to his American status. He also came armed with a whip, which he cracked every time he got off an epigram against Milton. He was a disciple of the philosopher Hulme, with whom he inaugurated imagism, intending to purify poetry of everything sentimental and rhetorical. In 1928 he was given the Dial Prize for his contribution to American letters. He lived in Rapallo, Italy, after 1924, where he was converted to fascism and contributed by lectures and on the radio to the spread of its doctrines. When the United States entered the war, he continued this activity. In 1946 he was brought back to his country and charged with treason. The court ruled that he was irresponsible, and he was shut up for some twelve years in a hospital for the insane. There are those who have seen this verdict as a stratagem to save him; others, as an accurate diagnosis. Despite all this he received the Bollingen Prize in 1949 for his *Pisan Cantos,* composed while he was imprisoned in Italy by the American army. Strangely, Pound believed that democracy as Jefferson understood it is not incompatible with fascism. He lived for a while in the castle of one of his daughters, who is married to an Italian aristocrat. He now lives in Venice.

Pound's work consists of poems, polemical essays, and translations from Chinese, Latin, Anglo-Saxon, Provençal, Italian, and French. The last have been severely criticized by scholars who seem not to have understood

Pound's purpose. For him the meaning of a text is less important than the sound of its words and the reproduction of its rhythm. Pound's major work is the *Cantos,* which he is now finishing and of which he has published more than a hundred. According to his exegetes, before Pound unity for a poet was the word; now it can be an extensive and irrelevant passage. Thus the first canto consists of a three-page translation in admirable free verse of a passage from book II of the *Odyssey,* together with an opinion regarding Guido Cavalcanti and interpretations of his work in Italian. The last cantos abound in citations from Confucius and contain some untranslated Chinese characters. This curious procedure has been defined as an amplification of the poetic unities. Pound declares that it was suggested to him by the ideograms of the Chinese writings in which a horizontal line above a circle represents the sunset: the horizontal line is the branch of a tree and the circle is the setting sun. The last cantos are less poetic than didactic. The work is difficult if not impossible to read. Pound indulges in unforeseen tenderness and at times in reminiscences of Whitman.

Thomas Stearns Eliot (1888–1965) was born in Saint Louis, Missouri, on the banks of the Mississippi, of which he would write: "The river is a strong brown god." His family came from New England. Eliot studied at Harvard, the Sorbonne, and Oxford. His work was published by reviews: the *Harvard Advocate* (1909–1910), *Poetry* (1915), the *Egoist* (1917), which became the voice of imagism, and finally *Criterion* (1922–1939), which he edited. He worked in Lloyd's Bank. In 1918 he tried unsuccessfully to enlist in the American navy. In 1927 he became a British subject. He returned after eighteen years to Harvard and held a chair of poetry. In 1922 he received the Dial Prize for the poem *The Waste Land* and in 1948 the Nobel Prize in Literature and the Order of Merit.

Eliot practiced literary criticism, the drama, and poetry, but when we think of him we are inclined to forget the multiplicity of his activities and to see him above all as a poet and critic. In his first critical essays, written in a very clear prose, he praised Ben Jonson, Donne, Dryden, and Matthew Arnold and attacked Milton and Shelley. These works exercised and continue to exercise a considerable influence, as does his long study of Dante. They helped Eliot to discover himself and were a stimulus to younger poets. In his essay on the potential of poetic drama he says that the work of the intelligence consists above all in purification, in abstention from reflection, in including in one's exposition enough to make reflection unnecessary. His theater, with perhaps the single exception of *Murder in the Cathedral,* leaves us with no vivid character. Eliot tried in one of his plays to create for our time a verse form of an almost oral liberty, something like that of the last period of Shakespeare and his followers Webster and Ford. He also employs classical elements such as the messenger and the chorus. In *The Family Reunion* the chorus plays a curious role, corresponding to the subconscious. The characters, who speak realistically, interrupt the dialogue to blurt out what they feel; then they take up the conversation again, unconscious of the strange verse they have recited. In *Murder in the Cathedral* the chorus declares the public's helplessness and forebodings with respect to the obscure will of the king and its tragic consequences. In the preface to his anthology of Ezra Pound, Eliot declares that the latter had his beginnings in Whitman, Browning, and the Provençal and Chinese poets, while he himself arrived at free verse from the reading of Laforgue and Tristan Corbière. The deserted land symbolizes *The Waste Land* (1922), a way of life from which the concept of good and evil has been excluded and which reflects the disillusionment of the years immediately following the war of 1918. *Ash Wednesday,* which appeared in 1930, is made up of six poems. The last lines, which show us the wind and the sea, but still without ships, signify the renunciation of the soul before the divine will. Perhaps the most important work of Eliot is his *Four Quartets,* brought together under this title in 1942. Though he began to publish them in 1940, they form a unity of affirmation rather than one of negation. The four titles are four places in England and America. The word *quartet* is not arbitrary; the structure of the four poems is the poetic equivalent of a sonata in which one can distinguish five movements. The central theme, already foreshadowed in *The Family Reunion,* is the Christian possibility of a fusion of the temporal with the eternal.

Eliot has defined himself as a classicist in literature, a monarchist in politics, and an Anglican in religion.

The poet Edward Estlin Cummings (1894–1963) was born in Cambridge, Massachusetts, and attended Harvard. During the First World War he was an ambulance driver in the French army; an administrative error led to his confinement for several months in a concentration camp. His most famous book, *The Enormous Room,* published in 1922, refers to this incarceration as if it were a pilgrimage and, with its stock of autobiographical incidents, is based on Bunyan's seventeenth-century Puritan allegory, *The Pilgrim's Progress.* The poetic work of Cummings abounds in eccentricities of all sorts and is published in many volumes. Let us recall here the beginning of one of his stanzas:

> *god's terrible face, brighter than a spoon,*
> *collects the image of one fatal word;*
> *so that my life (which liked the sun and the moon)*
> *resembles something that has not occurred:*
> *i am a birdcage without any bird,*
> *a collar looking for a dog.*

Born in 1891 in the borough of Brooklyn, New York, Henry Valentine Miller, like other modern American writers, has had a variety of firsthand experiences. He has been a clerk, a tailor, a postal employee, a stockbroker, the owner of a clandestine bar, a storyteller, a writer of advertising copy, and, paradoxically, a painter of watercolors. In 1928 he went to Europe with his second wife and returned there alone in 1930. After that he was a proofreader, a writer on salary, and a professor of English in Dijon. In 1932 he wrote *Tropic of Cancer,* which appeared in Paris in 1934 and the publication of which was to be forbidden in the United States because of its exuberant obscenity. In 1933 he stayed with Alfred Perles in Clichy, where he wrote *Black Spring,* which he published in Paris in 1936. He was influenced by an ample circle of writers, among them Blaise Cendrars and Céline. In 1939, while still in Paris, he finished and published his *Tropic of Capricorn.* That same year he traveled through Greece, which for him is a living country rather than an archeological museum. The Second World War caused his return to America in January 1940. The trip to Greece inspired the book *The Colossus of Maroussi* (1941). His life oscillates between the old world and the new; he is now living in California and devoting himself fully to writing and painting.

According to its author *Tropic of Cancer* is not a book but a libel, a prolonged insult to God and to man and his destiny. *Black Spring,* which consists of ten unrelated chapters, is a series of nightmares, burlesque exaggerations, vain affirmations, and explorations of himself, together with nostalgic memories of Brooklyn. *Tropic of Capricorn* is dominated by blackness: Mara, its heroine, is dark and is dressed in black; she is at once Circe, Lilith, and America incarnate in a proud, winged, and sensual woman, a demon who mutilates and annuls. She is surrounded by snakes, monsters, and machines. Miller throws himself into the river of destruction, led by a hope of rebirth. In *The Air Conditioned Nightmare* America is the nightmare with air conditioning; the author is enamored of its opposite, Paris and the Mediterranean regions. The trilogy *The Rosy Crucifixion (Sexus, Plexus,* and *Nexus*) consists of five volumes at once messianic and sardonic; the general theme is happiness and redemption through suffering. Judaism is one of the many obsessions that people his volumes.

Miller's entire work constitutes a vast, phantasmagoric autobiography not exempt from wilful trivialities and ugliness, among which there are at times magic flashes. Miller has been an anarchist, a pacifist, and an unbeliever in all politics. Will he continue to be so?

[10]

The Poets

In 1855 Walt Whitman had declared that his work was nothing but a collection of suggestions and notes and that the poets to come would justify it and fulfill it. His country was to wait half a century, lulled as it was by the delicate music of Tennyson and Swinburne, before taking up the inheritance of *Leaves of Grass*.

One of the first innovators was Edgar Lee Masters (1869–1950). He was born in Garnett, Kansas, practiced law in Chicago, and, after 1898, published poetic and dramatic books without attracting much attention. In 1915 his *Spoon River Anthology* made him suddenly famous. It was suggested to him by the casual reading of the *Greek Anthology*. The book, which is a sort of human comedy, is made up of 250 epitaphs, or rather the confessions of the dead of an obscure country town who reveal their intimate life to us. Here is Ann Rutledge, "Beloved in life of Abraham Lincoln, / Wedded to him, not through union, / But through separation." Here is the poet Petit, who, insensible to the life about him, makes up dusty triolets "while Homer and Whitman roared in the pines." Here is Benjamin Pantier, who was always sustained by love for his wife, who did not love him. The work is written in free verse and is the only important one which its author has left us.

Edward Arlington Robinson (1869–1935) was born in Head Tide, Maine, was educated at Harvard, and was a city inspector. Theodore Roosevelt, impressed by his poems, appointed him in 1905 to a position in the customs house. Robinson won the Pulitzer Prize three times—the first time in 1921 for a new edition of poems previously published beginning in 1898, the second time in 1924 for *The Man Who Died Twice,* and finally in 1927 for *Tristram,* which is part of a series of works on the legend of King Arthur. Much of his poetry, like that of Masters, consists of psychological portraits of imaginary persons, but Robinson's was done under the complex influence of Browning. His style is traditional; he is an eloquent poet in the good sense of the word. Now almost forgotten, except in histories of literature, he has been judged by the critic John Crowe Ransom to be one of the three major poets of North America between the years 1900 and 1950; the other two are T. S. Eliot and Robert Frost. In his work persists the Puritan severity which was to bring him later to a materialistic pessimism.

Without any doubt the most respected and beloved of the poets of his country, Robert Lee Frost (1875–1963) does not belong to the effusive tradition of Walt Whitman but to the more reticent though no less sensitive one of Emerson. Although he was born in San Francisco, California, he is by his background, character, and by the themes of his work a poet of New England, that is to say, of that part of the United States of most ancient and settled culture. He worked in a textile mill, went to Harvard, from which he did not graduate, and was successively a schoolteacher, shoemaker, journalist, and finally a farmer. In 1912 he settled with his family in England, where he became the friend of Rupert Brooke, Lascelles Abercrombie, and other poets. He discovered his vocation fairly late in life. His first important work, *North of Boston*, dates from 1914 and was published in England. This book, which brought him fame, was followed by many others. In 1915 he returned to the United States and was named professor of poetry at Harvard. North America already recognized in him her poet. He won the Pulitzer Prize in Poetry four times, in 1938 the medal of the American Academy of Arts and Letters, and in 1941 that of the Poetry Society of America. Sixteen universities conferred honorary degrees upon him.

Frost has been defined as the poet of the synecdoche, the rhetorical device which uses the part for the whole. Indeed there are compositions by Frost, trivial on first sight, which contain a complex meaning. They may therefore be read on several planes—the manifest one and the suggested or latent one. This procedure corresponds to understatement, the practice of holding something back, which is so characteristic of England and New England. He uses what is rural and ordinary to provide a brief but adequate hint of spiritual realities. He is at the same time tranquil and puzzling. Scorning free verse, he has always cultivated the classical forms, and he handles them with hidden mastery and no apparent effort. His poems are not obscure; each of the planes—which are implied and which we can interpret in one or more ways—satisfies our imagination, but their number is infinite. Thus for one reader "Acquainted with the Night" is a confession of long-hidden experiences in low quarters; for another the word *night* becomes a symbol not of evil but of wretchedness, death, and mystery. "Stopping by Woods on a Snowy Evening" relates a true or imaginary episode of undeniable visual grace; it is permissible to take it literally or as a long metaphor. The same thing may be said of the poem "The Road Not Taken," whose first verse describes a yellow wood which begins by being real and which finally becomes also a symbol of the nostalgia to be found in every choice.

With the death of Robert Frost, Carl Sandburg (1878–1967), who is in some ways the antithesis of Frost, is now the best-known poet in the United States, although some of his reputation is based on his monumental *Life of Abraham Lincoln,* in six volumes, which won him the Pulitzer Prize in 1940. The son of Swedish immigrants, he was born in Galesburg, Illinois. He was successively a milkman, a truckdriver, a bricklayer, a harvester, a dishwasher, a soldier in Puerto Rico during the war with Spain, a newspaperman, and a student of literature. His first work, *In Reckless Ecstasy,* published in 1904, found little acceptance. Ten years later he became famous through his contributions to Harriet Monroe's magazine *Poetry* in Chicago. In 1916 he brought out his *Chicago Poems.* He was awarded the prize of the American Poetry Society in 1919 and 1920. He then went about the country singing, reciting, and collecting popular songs, which he was to bring together in 1927 in *The American Songbag.* Among his many books we shall cite *Smoke and Steel* (1920), *Good Morning, America* (1928), and *The People, Yes* (1936). In 1950 his *Complete Poems* won him the Pulitzer Prize.

In all his work Whitman's influence is evident. Both poets handle free verse and slang, although Sandburg's use of the latter is richer and more spontaneous. He began as a poet of energy and even of violence and vulgarity; later he became one of melancholy and nostalgia. This process is to be seen in one of his most famous poems, "Cool Tombs."

A dweller in Illinois like Masters and Sandburg, Nicholas Vachel Lindsay (1879–1931) was born in Springfield, the hometown of Abraham Lincoln, for whom he shared their enthusiasm. He took courses at the Art Institute in Chicago; during the day he worked in a store. He continued his studies in art school in New York, but he could not sell his sketches. Then he tried poetry. Until 1913, when Harriet Monroe published his most famous poem, "General William Booth Enters into Heaven," he traveled about the Middle West on foot, earning his living as an entertainer, reciting his verse in exchange for board and room. In 1925 he married and went to live in Spokane, Washington; six years later he killed himself in Springfield. His works include *A Handy Guide for Beggars, The Chinese Nightingale, The Golden Whales of California,* and *Every Soul is a Circus.* Lindsay wanted to be the poet of the Salvation Army. He started to write a versified mythology of popular figures: Andrew Jackson, the hero of the War of 1812 and of the Indian Wars; the abolitionist John Brown; Lincoln; and Mary Pickford. His work is very uneven. In it we see the influence of jazz and the religious fervor of the spirituals. In certain poems the poet indicates what instruments and melody should accompany his words.

Up to now the contributions to poetry of American Negroes have been less important than their contributions to music. We shall cite first of all James Langston Hughes, born in Joplin, Missouri, in 1902, who, like Sandburg, is a literary descendant of Whitman. His work, which uses jazz rhythms, includes *Dear Lovely Death* [1931], *The Dream Keeper* [1932], *Shakespeare in Harlem* [1942], *One Way Ticket* [1949], and his autobiography, *The Big Sea* [1940]. His verses contain pathos and are not seldom sardonic.

More carefully composed and more sensitive is the work of Countee Cullen (1903–1946), who was educated in New York, his native city, and at Harvard. Among other books he published *Copper Sun, The Black Christ,* and a version of the *Medea* of Euripides. He compiled two anthologies of Negro poetry, but racial concerns interested him less than intimate ones. Critics have noted in him the influence of Keats.

[11]

The Novel

In contrast to American writers who came to literature by way of an adventurous life, John Phillips Marquand, born in Wilmington, Delaware, in 1893, was brought up in the intellectual atmosphere of a distinguished New England family. He was a grandnephew of the transcendentalist Margaret Fuller; his wife belonged to an old Boston family. He went to Harvard, was an artilleryman during the First World War, and practiced journalism. His best novel, *The Late George Apley,* ironically reflects the refined atmosphere of Boston. He also tried his hand at detective stories.

More varied was the career of Louis Bromfield (1896–1956). His father was a farmer in Ohio. Bromfield attended Cornell and Columbia universities. He lived in France on a rural property near Senlis. During the First World War he drove an ambulance and won the Croix de Guerre. He was a drama critic and journalist. In 1926 *Early Autumn,* part of a chronicle of a family of industrialists, won the Pulitzer Prize. His work is extensive; other novels are *When the Rains Came* (1937), which was adapted for a movie, *Night in Bombay* (1940), and *Mrs. Parkington* [1942].

Of German and Irish origin, John Ernest Steinbeck was born in Salinas, California, in 1902. To earn his expenses at Stanford University he took various jobs: he was a laboratory worker in a sugar refinery, a bricklayer, a domestic servant, and a newspaperman.

At twenty-seven he began his literary career with the publication of a novel about the pirate Morgan, *Cup of Gold*. Of his abundant later work we shall recall *Of Mice and Men* (1937); the series of stories *The Long Valley* (1938), which includes "The Red Pony"; *The Grapes of Wrath* [1939], which won the Pulitzer Prize; and *East of Eden* (1952). Some of these books inspired famous films. The scene of almost all his books is California; their humble setting reflects the results of the Depression of 1930. Steinbeck is outstanding in dialogue, in the description of the life he has known, and in narrative; he is less satisfactory when he undertakes philosophical or social problems.

It has been said of the picaresque novel that it is a literature of hunger; the same thing, with greater intensity, would apply to the work of Erskine Caldwell, except that in his work hunger, an erotic frenzy, and a kind of animal innocence are brought together to exclude all feelings of guilt. Like Faulkner, Caldwell describes the decadence of the South after the War of the Secession, but his characters are not aristocrats who have had a comedown but poor whites doomed to grow tobacco and cotton in worn-out soil. The son of a Presbyterian minister, Erskine Preston Caldwell was born in White Oak, Georgia, in 1903. He studied at the Universities of Virginia and Pennsylvania and worked at various jobs like so many other American writers. In 1926 he retired to an abandoned farm to learn the art of writing. There he wrote his famous novel *Tobacco Road* (1932), which was dramatized and played for several years. This work shows us human beings reduced to elementary necessities—eating, cohabiting, working the land. The atrocious is mingled with the comic and the grotesque. *God's Little Acre* has been judged Caldwell's best novel; the reader can sympathize with his characters. In his book of short stories, *We Are the Living,* the author's art shows itself as more direct and sober and less uninhibited.

Far more complex than the writers thus far considered is Robert Penn Warren, novelist, poet, critic, professor, and storyteller. He was born in Guthrie, Kentucky, in 1905. He studied at Yale and then at Oxford. He has been a professor of English at the universities of Louisiana and Minnesota. In 1942 he won the Shelley Prize for poetry. He edited the *Southern Review;* in 1950 he became a professor in the department of dramatic art at Yale. In his youth he belonged to a group of regional writers. His poetry, admirably executed, varies from the narrative and popular to the philosophical and reflective. In it has been seen the influence of the English metaphysical poets of the seventeenth century. His novels include *All the King's Men* (1946), which earned him the Pulitzer Prize, *Night Rider* (1939), *All Heaven's Gate* (1943), and *World Enough and Time* (1950), whose title is taken from the first line of a poem by Andrew Marvell. *Circus in the Attic* (1948) is a collection of short stories.

The Negro novelist Richard Wright was born on a plantation near Natchez, Mississippi, in 1908. His father had abandoned the family; Richard Wright's upbringing was provided partly by an orphan asylum and partly by relatives. At fifteen he was a postal employee in Memphis. After that he lived in Chicago and New York, and since 1946 he has lived in Paris. In 1938 he published a series of stories, *Uncle Tom's Children,* which won him a fifty-dollar prize. His greatest successes were perhaps *Native Son* (1940), the story of an involuntary crime and its tremendous consequences; his autobiography, *Black Boy,* published in 1945; and *Twelve Million Black Voices* (1941), which applies naturalistic techniques to racial conflict. In 1940 he won the Spingarn Medal, the highest reward given for a work on behalf of Negroes. In Paris he published, among other books, *How I Tried to Be a Communist* and *The Outsider* (1952), in which, under Sartre's influence, he moves from the specific problem of being a Negro to the fundamental problem of being a man. This transition does not imply a rupture with his previous work; in both stages his subject is always man harassed by a hostile society. He was a Marxist in Chicago; his present work reflects his disillusionment with the hope for universal brotherhood, which he expected to find in communism, and his search for other ideals. The novel *Native Son* has been adapted to the screen.

Truman Streckfus Persons, famous under the name Truman Capote, was born in New Orleans, Louisiana, in 1925. He studied in Connecticut. He was successively a scenario writer, a dancer on a river boat, and a writer for the *New Yorker.* At nineteen he won the O. Henry Prize with his story "Miriam"; the same prize was conferred on him again in 1948 for "Shut a Final Door." Random House published his series of short stories, *Tree of Night*

(1949). His first novel, *Other Voices, Other Rooms,* of 1948, which many people thought autobiographical, made him famous. In 1951 he published *The Grass Harp,* which he had written in Sicily and the partial truth of which was suspected by no one. He twice attempted the theater with but scant success. In 1956 he published *Muses Are Heard,* which tells about his trip to the Soviet Union, accompanying a production of *Porgy and Bess.*

The story told in his most recent book, *In Cold Blood* (1966) is a strange one. A quadruple murder had been committed in a Kansas town. Truman Capote, whose chief preoccupation thus far had been with style, used this frightful crime to create a new literary form, which partakes of both journalism and literature. He moved to Kansas, where he was to remain for five years. He questioned everyone in the vicinity and won the confidence and friendship of the murderers, whom he continued to interview until the hour of their execution by hanging and who bade him an affectionate farewell. He wanted to find out how a man comes to commit a crime. He felt intuitively that the act of notetaking inhibits the person questioned, and so he trained himself to memorize everything the murderers told him. *In Cold Blood* is composed with an almost inhuman objectivity which recalls certain literary experiments tried in France.

[12]

The Theater

It is odd that in England, the land of Shakespeare, the drama was singularly poor during the nineteenth century until Shaw and Oscar Wilde revitalized it. Something similar occurred in North America. There was a popular theater, and distinguished authors produced plays less intended to be played than to be read. We cite in England the cases of Tennyson and Browning and in the United States that of Longfellow.

Eugene Gladstone O'Neill (1888–1953) was born in New York, the son of a romantic actor who achieved a certain notoriety. Of Irish descent, he was educated in Catholic boarding schools in various cities and finally at Princeton. His life was adventurous and contradictory. A goldseeker in Honduras, a sailor on American and Norwegian ships, a vagabond in the back alleys of Buenos Aires, a laborer in Berisso, an actor and a newspaperman, he was nonetheless an assiduous reader of Greek tragedies and of Ibsen and Strindberg. He won the Pulitzer Prize four times and in 1936 the Nobel. He was married three times, and his daughter Oona is the wife of [Charlie] Chaplin.

No less varied than his life is his work, which consists of more than thirty plays and an autobiography. His writing moves from realism to expressionism and abounds in curious experiments, whose boldness is generally justified by success. Thus in *Where the Cross Is Made* (1918) a hallucinatory vision of the bottom of the sea and of dead sailors appears in a New England house. In *The Great God Brown* (1926) his use of symbolic masks, which the characters put on and take off and with which they speak, without realizing that they are doing so, produces an effect of terror; the mask replaces the man and can be loved or hated. In *Strange Interlude* (1927) O'Neill brought back the aside, or monologue, making it coincide with the stream of consciousness as in the final chapter of Joyce's *Ulysses*. His trilogy, *Mourning Becomes Electra,* transmutes the ancient legend to the years of the Civil War. It cannot be denied that beyond our preferences or antipathies O'Neill has renewed the dramatic technique of our times. His tormented spirit is reflected in his work, which always excludes the happy ending. He has been translated into nearly all languages. His early plays, which were usually limited to a single act, were first put on by small groups of experimenters, such as the Washington Square Players, the Provincetown Players, and the Experimental Theater, in whose management he took part. They then reached Broadway and the rest of the world.

The son of a newspaperman who became consul-general in Hong Kong, Thornton Niven Wilder was born in Madison, Wisconsin, in 1897. He studied extensively in China, California, and at Oberlin and Yale. After graduating he took courses in archeology at the American Academy in Rome and at Princeton. During the First World War he served in the artillery, during the Second in the air force. From 1921 to 1928 he was a teacher of French at Lawrenceville Academy. His first novel, *The Cabala,* appeared in 1926; *The Bridge of San Luis Rey* (1927) gave him world fame and a Pulitzer Prize. Among his other novels are *The Woman of Andros* (1930), *Heaven's My Destination* (1934), and *The Ides of March* (1948).

In Wilder's dramatic work technical innovations which surprise the spectator are probably less important than emotion, a sense of the humane, optimism, and intelligence. To that we can add a sense of the passage of time derived from his archeological studies. He began with very short plays, of ten minutes duration, which put scriptural themes into a contemporary mold. In *Our Town* (1938) the world of the dead is no less real than that of the living, and the author finds essential value in trivial daily acts. *The Skin of Our Teeth* (1942) brings together on a single plane prehistoric and contemporary events. The dinosaur and the mammoth walk across the stage complaining of the cold, and the Antrobus family burns its furniture and papers to warm the children. Thornton Wilder has remarked that the novel corresponds to a time that is past, the theater to present time. In the theater the time is always now.

Of Armenian descent, William Saroyan was born in Fresno, California, in 1908. He lived that many-sided life that seems to be a tradition with American writers. He was a postal clerk, an office boy, and a farmhand. Then he settled in San Francisco. He has divided his literary activity among the novel, the short story, and the theater, to which he owes his principal fame. The characters in his comedies—as for example *My Heart's in the High-*

lands and *The Time of Your Life,* both of 1939—are vagabonds, prostitutes, drunkards, and the dispossessed. Saroyan, like Dickens, is less interested in the misfortunes of the poor than in their courage, their kindness, their hopes, and their fleeting joys. *The Time of Your Life* won him the Pulitzer Prize. No less famous is the comedy *The Beautiful People,* which had its first performance two years later. These plays were all conceived of as poems or as music. There is almost no plot; what is essential are states of mind, an anarchic and generous romanticism. We find these same traits in his novels and short stories. He began his writing career in 1934 with a book of short stories, *The Daring Young Man on the Flying Trapeze,* which was followed, among others, by *The Human Comedy* [1943] and the autobiography *The Bicycle Rider in Beverly Hills* (1952). He wrote that he believed more in dreams than in statistics. In his disdain for the well-constructed work the influence of Sherwood Anderson has been seen. He greatly admired Bernard Shaw and wrote, like him, long prefaces for his plays. In one of them he says: "In the time of your life, live—so that in that good time there shall be no ugliness or death for yourself or for any life your life touches. Seek goodness everywhere and when it is found bring it out of its hiding place and let it be free and unashamed."

The son of a traveling salesman, Thomas Lanier Williams, who would become famous under the name Tennessee Williams, was born in 1914 in the state of Mississippi. He was educated at the Universities of Missouri and Iowa. In 1940 he won a Rockefeller scholarship. Then he worked for a movie company in Hollywood, where he was to write his first successful play, *The Glass Me-*

nagerie (1945). After this came *A Streetcar Named Desire* (1947) and *Summer and Smoke* (1949). From his many-faceted work, which runs the gamut of the themes of decadence, poverty, carnal instincts, covetousness, mutilation, incest, and frustration seeking refuge in an imaginary life, we shall recall only a few titles: *The Rose Tattoo* (1950), *Cat on a Hot Tin Roof* (1955), *Suddenly Last Summer* [1958], and *Sweet Bird of Youth* (1959). From all these plays, in which materialism and anguish coexist with psychoanalysis, without a breath of hope, *Camino Real* [1953] differs, or at least tries to differ. This is an ambitious allegorical effort whose characters include Lord Byron, Casanova, Don Quixote, Sancho, and the *Dame aux Camélias*. Of these works many have been adapted as motion pictures.

Arthur Miller, whose name is frequently associated with that of Tennessee Williams, was born in New York in 1915. In 1938 he graduated from the University of Michigan. While still very young, he began to write for the theater. Differing from other social dramatists, who attribute everything to environment, Miller believes in free will. He won his first success with *All My Sons,* which dates from 1947. Its hero owes his fortune to the sale of defective airplanes. His son, who considers him guilty of the death of many soldiers, resolves to crash his plane on his last flight; when the father learns this he also decides to commit suicide. In 1949 occurred the première of the now famous play *Death of a Salesman.* Its hero, Willy Loman, loses his job after more than thirty years' work. He decides to let himself be killed in an automobile accident so that his family may collect his insurance. In this drama the present and the past are mingled in the manner of Faulkner. In *The Crucible* (1953) Miller strives for a double effect; the ostensible theme is the witch trials of Salem, which occurred in the last decade of the seventeenth century, but the audience feels that the play also implies an attack on the persecutions and fanaticisms of the contemporary world. *A View from the Bridge* [1955] is a brief tragedy whose locale is the docks of New York. The action occurs in the memory of one of the characters, the lawyer Alfieri. *A Memory of Two Mondays* was first performed in 1955. The characters vegetate in a sordid atmosphere of routine and poverty from which only one, a young man, succeeds in escaping to try other paths. Arthur Miller was the husband of the famous actress Marilyn Monroe; it is supposed that the subject of *The Fall* [1964] was inspired by his wife's fate. His plays have been turned into many films. In 1945 he wrote the novel *Focus,* an attack on anti-Semitism.

[13]

The Detective Story,
Science Fiction,
& the Far West

In 1840 Edgar Allan Poe enriched literature with a new genre. This genre is above all ingenious and artificial; real crimes are not commonly discovered by abstract reasoning but by chance, investigation, or confession. Poe invented the first detective in literature, M. Charles Auguste Dupin of Paris. He invented at the same time the convention, later classical, that the exploits of the hero should be told by an admiring and mediocre friend. Let us recall the later Sherlock Holmes and his biographer, Doctor Watson. Poe left five stories of the detective type, all unsurpassed, according to Chesterton. In the first, "The Murders in the Rue Morgue," he is investigating the frightful murder of two women in an apparently locked garret. The guilty one is an orangoutang. "The Purloined Letter" originates the idea of hiding a precious object in plain view of everyone so that no one will no-tice it. "The Mystery of Marie Roget" is reduced to an abstract discussion of the probable solution of a crime, without any adventure whatsoever. In "Thou Art the Man" the guilty man, as in a certain story by Israel Zangwill, is the detective himself. In "The Gold Bug" the investigator deciphers a cryptogram which will reveal the precise location of a hidden treasure. Poe has had many imitators; let it suffice to mention for the moment his contemporary, Dickens, and Stevenson and Chesterton.

The intellectual tradition initiated by Edgar Allan Poe has found more classic successors in England than in his own country. We shall recall a few names of Americans.

Willard Huntington Wright (1888–1939) was born in Charlottesville, Virginia. He studied at California and Harvard, in Paris and Munich. With Mencken and Nathan he edited the famous magazine *Smart Set*. His literary destiny is curious; his serious books, *What Nietzsche Taught, Modern Painting,* and *The Future of Painting,* are forgotten today; the detective novels, which he wrote to distract himself during a convalescence, made him famous. He published them under the pseudonym S. S. Van Dine. Let us recall *The Benson Murder Case, The Canary Murder Case,* and *Murder in the Casino.* His hero, Philo Vance, is by his urbanity and pedantry an evident projection of the author himself.

Erle Stanley Gardner was born in 1889 in Malden, Massachusetts.[29] Like Jack London he was a prospector in Alaska. He was admitted to the bar in California, where he was preeminent in his profession for more than twenty years. Perry Mason, the principal character in his long series of novels, is also a lawyer. We shall cite *The Deaf and Dumb Bishop, The Lame Canary, The Musical*

Cow, The Cadaver in Flight, Imperfect Assassination, and *The Nervous Accomplice.* His works have been translated into sixteen languages. His fame in the United States has surpassed that of Conan Doyle. He has also often used the pseudonym A. A. Fair.

Frederick Dannay and his cousin Lee Manfred have made famous the pseudonym Ellery Queen, who is at the same time the author and the protagonist of their novels, which are told in the third person. They began their combined career with *The Roman Hat Mystery* (1929), which won a prize. Of their many books we shall mention *The Egyptian Cross Mystery, The Chinese Orange Mystery, The Greek Coffin Mystery, The Siamese Twin Mystery, The Spanish Cape Mystery.* Their books are distinguished by scrupulous honesty, vivid dramatic treatment, and ingenious solutions to the problems. They have been praised by Priestley.

Dashiell Hammett was born in Maryland in 1894. He was a news vendor, a messenger, a stevedore, a publicity agent, and for seven years a detective in the famous Pinkerton agency. Until his appearance the detective story had been abstract and intellectual; Hammett acquaints us with the reality of the criminal world and of police work. His detectives are no less violent than the outlaws whom they pursue. Let us cite *Red Harvest* (1929), *The Dain Curse, The Maltese Falcon* [1930], *The Glass Key* [1931], and *The Thin Man* [1932]. The atmosphere of his works is disagreeable.[30]

The detective novel has gradually been displaced by the novel of espionage and by science fiction. Certain stories of E. A. Poe ("The Case of Mr. Valdemar," "The Global Mystification") already prefigure this last category, but its outstanding creators are European: in France Jules Verne, whose anticipations have largely proved prophetic, in England H. G. Wells, whose books have much of the nightmare about them. K[ingsley] Amis has defined science fiction thus: "It is a story in prose whose circumstances could not arise in the world as we know it, but the basis of which is the hypothesis of an innovation of some sort, of human or extra-terrestrial origin, in the field of science and technology, or, one might say, in the field of pseudo-science or pseudo-technology."

The first media of distribution for science fiction were magazines, not books. In April 1911 there appeared in *Modern Electrics* the serial "Ralph 124 C 4: Novel of the Year 1966." The founder of the magazine, Hugo Gernsback, wrote it, and it won the Hugo Prize created later, which still recalls his name and which is intended for this sort of writing. In 1926 Gernsback founded *Amazing Stories;* at present there are in the United States more than twenty similar magazines. This is not a popular genre; its readers are usually engineers, chemists, men of science, technologists, and students, with a noticeable predominance of men. Their enthusiasm sometimes leads them to form clubs which bridge all social levels and which are counted by the dozens. One of these organizations is called, not without humor, "The Little Monsters of America."

Howard Philips Lovecraft (1890–1937) was born in Providence, Rhode Island. Very sensitive and of delicate health, he was educated by his widowed mother and aunts. Like Hawthorne he enjoyed solitude, and although he worked during the day, he did so with the shades lowered.

In 1924 he married and moved to Brooklyn; in 1929 he was divorced and returned to Providence, where he went back to his life of solitude. He died of cancer. He detested the present and professed a fondness for the eighteenth century.

Science attracted him: his first article had to do with astronomy. He published but a single book during his lifetime; after his death his friends brought together in book form the considerable body of his work, which had been dispersed in anthologies and magazines. He studiously imitated the style of Poe with its sonorities and pathos, and he wrote comic nightmares. In his stories one meets beings from remote planets and from ancient or future epochs who dwell in human bodies to study the universe or, conversely, souls of our time who during sleep explore monstrous worlds, distant in time and space. Among his works we shall recall "The Color from Space," "The Dunwich Horror," and "The Rats in the Wall."

He also left a voluminous correspondence. To Poe's influence upon him one should also add that of the visionary storyteller Arthur Machen.

Robert Heinlein was born in Fulton, Missouri, in 1907. His life has been extremely varied; he has tried aviation, the navy, physics, chemistry, real estate, politics, architecture, and, since 1934, writing. His precarious health has obliged him to make frequent changes. Heinlein thinks that after poetry science fiction is the most difficult of literary genres and the only one capable of reflecting the genuine spirit of our times. His varied work is mainly intended for young people. He has attempted radio, television, and movies. Of his work, which has been translated into many languages, we shall mention the following titles: *Beyond the Horizon* (1948), *Red Planet* (1949), *Farmer in the Sky* [1950], *The Man Who Sold the Moon* (1950), *Between the Planets* (1951), and *Assignment in Eternity* [1953].

Of Dutch descent, Alfred Elton Van Vogt was born in Canada in 1912. He grew up on the plains of Saskatchewan; from earliest childhood he had a strange conviction of being a common person surrounded by other common persons, far from all possible greatness. At twelve he started his literary career with the publication of an autobiographical story, and this was followed by others of similar or sentimental character. Science fiction always attracted him, but his first attempts at the genre date from 1939. One of his favorite subjects is the man who does not know who he is and who goes in search of himself without entirely succeeding. The mechanical interests him less than the mental. His work is inspired by mathematics, logic, semantics, cybernetics, and hypnosis. Of his stories we shall mention *Slan* (1946); *The Book of Ptah* (1948), an epic of an imaginary planet; and *The World of Null Ā* (1948), based on general semantics. In collaboration with Hedna May Hull, his wife, he wrote *Out of the Unknown* (1948).

Ray Bradbury has won greater fame than the foregoing. He was born in Waukegan, Illinois, in 1920. From childhood the adventures of Tarzan and the practice of sleight of hand had accustomed him to living in a world of fantasy. His early reading of *Amazing Stories* led him to science fiction. At twelve he was given a typewriter as a present. In 1935, while still in school, he took a course on the technique of fiction. From then on he made a practice of writing one or two thousand words a day. Beginning in 1941 he contributed to several magazines of the class of *American Mercury*. In 1946 he won a prize offered by *The Best American Short Stories,* which had been the ideal of his childhood. His first book, *Dark Carnival,* dates from 1947; *Martian Chronicles* from 1950; *The Illustrated Man* from 1951; *Fahrenheit 451* from 1953; *The Golden Apples of the Sun,* whose title is taken from Yeats, from 1953; *Switch on the Night* from 1955. These books have been translated into nearly all languages.

"Science fiction is a marvelous hammer. I intend to use it to enable men to live as they wish," Bradbury has written. Amis, who criticizes Bradbury's sentimentality, admits his literary excellence and ironic force. Bradbury sees in the conquest of space an extension of mechanization and the tedium of our contemporary culture. In his work nightmares and occasionally cruelty appear, but above all sadness. The future that he anticipates has nothing utopian about it; he warns rather of dangers that humanity can and must avoid.

Let us now turn to the Western. Although of a different lineage, the cowboy must not have differed greatly from the gaucho. Both were horsemen of the plains; both had to contend with the Indians, the rigors of the desert, and untamed cattle. They shed their blood in wars which they probably never understood. Despite this fundamental identity the literatures which they have inspired are quite different. For Argentine writers—recalling *Martin Fierro*[31] and the novels of Eduardo Gutierrez[32]—the gaucho is the incarnation of rebellion and not infrequently of crime; in contrast the ethical preoccupation of North

Americans, based on Protestantism, has led them to present in the cowboy the triumph of good over evil. The gaucho of the literary tradition is usually a man of cunning; the cowboy may well be a sheriff or rancher. Both characters are now legendary. The motion picture has spread the myth of the cowboy throughout the world; oddly enough, Italy and Japan have taken up the production of western movies, which are quite alien to their history and culture.

The literature of the cowboy had its humble origin in the dime novels, whose circulation began in 1850 and lasted until the end of the century. The topics of the dime novels were historical, and their style was generally similar to the romantic manner of Dumas. When they had exhausted the history of the colonies, the Revolutionary War, and the Civil War, they took up the winning of the West. The cowboy then emerged as the figure representing the frontier.

Among those who cultivated this genre the best known is Zane Grey (1875–1939). He was born in Zanesville, Ohio. The son of a lumberman, he was educated at the University of Pennsylvania and practiced dentistry before devoting himself to writing. His first publications date from 1904. Of the sixty novels which he left behind we shall mention *The Last of the Plainsmen* (1909), *Desert Gold* (1913), and *The Mysterious Rider* (1921). Many of these books were turned into movies. Of his work, which has been translated into nearly all languages and which is still widely read, especially by children and young people, more than thirteen million copies have been sold.

In contrast to the *poesía gauchesca*[33] which came into

existence shortly after the revolution of 1810, the North American Western is a tardy and subordinate genre. One must admit, however, that it is a branch of the epic and that the brave and noble cowboy has become a worldwide symbol.

[14]

The Oral Poetry
of the Indians

It is probably to be regretted that the best anthology of this poetry in English, *The Path on the Rainbow,* edited by George Cronyn, dates from 1918, the date corresponding to the diffusion of the imagist school. The influence of this school upon the translators seems to be evident, except that we can also postulate a retrospective influence of Ezra Pound on the Indians. Be that as it may, to translate a poem is to transfer it not only to a different idiom but also to other historic circumstances and to another culture.

The poetry which *The Path on the Rainbow* offers to our curiosity surprises by its contemplative perception of the visual world, its delicacy, its magic, and its terseness. There are compositions that consist of a single verse, for instance, this charm by a medicine man:

> *Death I make, singing.*

Or:

> *Are they men or gods who come from the forest?*

Or these lines spoken by an Indian as he dies:

> *All my life*
> *I have been seeking,*
> *Seeking.*
> *In magic songs, man is one with divinity.*
> *It is I who wear the morning star on my head.*

Philologists have not yet discovered the metrics of the Indian; each poem corresponds to a dance and includes meaningless syllables. By its diverse rhythm the hearers can tell whether a song is a love song, an epic song, or a magic song, even if they do not understand the language. The metaphors are not logically justified but they are effective; one song invokes the silver foxes of the moon.

We have spoken of charms which can cause a man's death; the Irish also attributed that power to satire. The Indians had songs to effect cures, songs to arouse love, and songs to bring victory. They composed songs that a man could only confide to another man at the hour of death. As Baudelaire has it, these things are like the echo of an absent, a distant and almost dead world.

Finally let us cite this song of the Navajos:

> *The magpie! the magpie! Here underneath*
> *In the white of his wings are the footsteps of morning.*
> *It dawns! it dawns!*

Judging by the testimony of Parkman,[34] based on translations, the Iroquois cultivated successfully the art of political oratory.

Appendix

Some Historic Dates

1584 Founding of the ill-fated Roanoke Colony in North Carolina.

1607 Founding of Jamestown by the Virginia Company of London.

1619 Arrival in a Dutch boat of the first Negro slaves.

1620 Founding of Plymouth Colony (Massachusetts) by the Pilgrims of the Mayflower.

1664 The British capture Dutch New Amsterdam (New York).

1754–1760 French and Indian wars. Defeat of the French. Ceding of French territory.

1775–1783 War of the American Revolution. Independence of the colonies.

1787 Constitutional Convention in Philadelphia.

1789–1797 Presidency of George Washington.

1801–1809 Presidency of Thomas Jefferson.

1803 Acquisition from France of Louisiana Territory.

1812–1814 War with England.

1823 The Monroe Doctrine.

1829–1837 Presidency of Andrew Jackson.

1836 Texas declaration of independence.

1845 Annexation of Texas by the United States.

91

1846–1848 War with Mexico.

1856 Organization of the Republican party.

1861–1865 Presidency of Abraham Lincoln (assassinated). War of the Secession. Defeat of the South.

1867 Acquisition of Alaska from Russia.

1869–1877 Presidency of General Ulysses S. Grant (Republican).

1896 Discovery of gold in the Klondike.

1898 War with Spain.

1901–1909 Presidency of Theodore Roosevelt (Republican).

1913–1921 Presidency of Woodrow Wilson (Democrat). Entry of the United States into the First World War, April 6, 1917.

1921–1923 Presidency of Warren G. Harding (Republican).

1923–1929 Presidency of Calvin Coolidge (Republican).

1929 Economic depression.

1933–1946 Presidency of Franklin D. Roosevelt (Democrat). New Deal. Entry of the United States into the Second World War, December 1941.

1953–1961 Presidency of General Dwight D. Eisenhower (Republican).

1961–1963 Presidency of John F. Kennedy, (Democrat, assassinated). Alliance for Progress.

1963 Presidency of Lyndon B. Johnson (Democrat).

Notes

[1] Ricardo Güiraldes, 1886–1927. Distinguished Argentine writer.

[2] Rubén Darío, 1867–1916. Influential Nicaraguan poet.

[3] Leopoldo Lugones, 1874–1938. Argentine poet and novelist.

[4] Pablo Neruda, b. 1904. Chilean poet.

[5] Edwards, it appears, began as an idealist, independent of but not very different from Berkeley. His theology progressed until he espoused a view of supernatural conversion that caused him to withhold Communion from those who had not had that experience. He attacked Arminianism and came in time to a view of God as Love which tended to negate the personal, Hebraic conception. In this respect he perhaps foreshadows the transcendentalists and is a precursor of Emerson's concept of the Oversoul.

[6] The term *Brahmin* is applicable to Edwards; however, it is perhaps worth noting that its use in literary histories is usually reserved for the later, transcendentalist writers, such as Emerson.

[7] A notable omission at this point from the perspective of North American literature as taught in the United States is the name of Thomas Paine, the political propagandist.

[8] Diego Sarmiento, 1811–1888. As suggested, he was, like Franklin, a universal genius. He was a scholar, teacher, and president of Argentina.

[9] *Facundo,* his great work, is a philosophical study of dictatorship.

[10] *Eripuit coelo fulmen, sceptrumque tyrannis.*

[11] Borges may be slightly misleading. Cooper continued to practice the craft of the novelist while in Europe and in fact composed part at least of *The Water Witch* while staying at the Hotel Tramontano in Sorrento (the house in which Tasso was born). The book, however, is set in the region of New York City.

[12] Most of Cooper's hostility to Europe seems to have arisen after his return to the United States.

[13] For example, "The Murders in the Rue Morgue," "The Purloined Letter."

[14] It is possible that Thoreau's importance as a political thinker has not yet had its full impact on society. His intricate symbolism, both in the prose, which is sometimes ornate and sometimes quite plain, and in the poetry, which Borges does not discuss, may have delayed the full impact of his ideas.

[15] Jorge Manrique (1440?–1479). Outstanding poet of the reign of Henry IV. His *Coplas a la muerte del Maestre de Santiago,* an elegy in forty stanzas, is an excellent specimen of medieval Spanish poetry.

[16] An intended transliteration of the Argentine *gaucho,* cowboy.

[17] Brown is correct, but he neglects to note, as does Borges, that the theme was earlier voiced by Thoreau.

[18] Matthiessen in *The American Renaissance* points out that explanations of the white whale have become a sort of parlor game among scholars.

[19] Borges is not entirely fair to Zola, who documented his work in libraries but is also famous for having supposedly thrown himself under the wheels of a carriage to ascertain what it felt like to be run over.

[20] Lanier's work on prosody here referred to is *The Science of English Verse* (1880); while it is true that the insistence is on time as opposed to stress, the argument is too fuzzy to be worth much except as a curiosity. Subsequent works such as Thomson's *The Rhythm of Speech* and Croll's *The Rhythm of English Verse* entirely supersede Lanier.

[21] It should be pointed out that the poem is open to other, dif-

ferent interpretations; it could possibly refer to the death of a member of her family.

[22] Argentine dictator, 1793–1877.

[23] Both are realists, or, if you like, one is a realist and one a naturalist; hence there is a relationship between them that transcends matters of influence.

[24] The theme of money, common to naturalistic literature, appears in both Norris and Dreiser. Regardless of what he may have been "at heart," Dreiser is usually thought of as an American naturalist.

[25] Dos Passos died on 28 September 1970.

[26] Faulkner created a mythical place, like Sidney's Arcadia or Spenser's Faerieland—a major literary accomplishment.

[27] More accurately, Hemingway enlisted as a volunteer ambulance driver in France and was transferred to the Italian front.

[28] The work that served as an immediate occasion for the prize was *The Old Man and the Sea;* it was thought at the time that the committee honored Hemingway belatedly and for an inferior work, though critical opinion of the work has varied since then.

[29] Gardner died on 11 March 1970.

[30] The atmosphere was not always disagreeable; *The Thin Man,* for example, contains charming people in a charming and urbane atmosphere.

[31] Argentine epic by José Fernández, part I published in 1872, part II in 1879.

[32] 1853–1889. Also author of the great play of the Argentine theatre, *Juan Moreira* (1886).

[33] Poetry inspired by the exploits of the gaucho.

[34] Reference is to Francis Parkman (1823–1893), author of *The Oregon Trail* and numerous other works; Borges does not say which passage he had in mind.